"A hard hitting job search manual that stands out from the pack. A must for anyone who wants to get a running start on a successful job search."

**—William H. (Mo) Marumoto
Chairman of the Board, The Interface Group, Ltd.**

"A valuable addition to a job seeker's education on how to sell themselves on paper."

**—Richard C. Slayton
President, Slayton International, Inc.**

"Thanks to Loretta Foxman's expert presentation of street-smart job search strategies, job seekers of every stripe—whether recent grads or seasoned executives—can fact today's sagging job market with skill and confidence."

Marilyn Moats Kennedy, Editor/Publisher
Kennedy's Career Strategist

RESUMES THAT WORK
HOW TO SELL YOURSELF ON PAPER

Second Edition

Loretta D. Foxman
edited by Walter L. Polsky

John Wiley & Sons, Inc.
New York • Chichester • Brisbane • Toronto • Singapore

To my father, Frederick Foxman

who dreamed of wonderful things
for all seven of his children

who taught us to seek
knowledge and excellence

who showed us the way
of kindness and generosity

who believed in us
and helped us believe in ourselves

In recognition of the importance of preserving what has been written, it is a policy of John Wiley & Sons, Inc., to have books of enduring value published in the United States printed on acid-free paper, and we exert our best efforts to that end.

Copyright © 1993 by Loretta D. Foxman

Published by John Wiley & Sons, Inc.

Library of Congress Cataloging-in-Publication Data

Foxman, L. D. (Loretta D.)
    Resumes that work : how to sell yourself on paper / Loretta D.
  Foxman ; edited by Walter L. Polsky. — 2nd ed.
      p.   cm.
    Rev. ed. of: The key to your successful resume. c 1982.
    Includes bibliographical references.
    ISBN 0-471-57747-2 (pbk.)
    1. Résumés (Employment)   I. Polsky, Walter L.   II. Foxman, L. D.
  (Loretta D.).   Key to your successful resume.   III. Title.
  HF5383.F82   1993
  808'.06665—dc20   92-20595

10 9 8 7 6 5 4 3 2 1

CONTENTS

vi CONTENTS

FOREWORD

Few major American companies survived the late eighties and early nineties intact. Restructurings designed to boost sagging bottom lines gutted management layers at organizations large and small. While the majority of laid-off managers and executives have landed positions with other employers (some at lower salaries and with fewer responsibilities, perhaps by choice), others struggle to find the right opportunities.

The reshaping of corporate organizational charts and subsequent travails of laid-off executives have created a dire need for intelligent career advice. Many services have emerged to fill the gap, ranging from company-paid outplacement programs to private counselors to inexpensive job clubs. Yet the greatest growth seems to be on the shelves of local bookstores. It's there that literally thousands of job-search and career-guidance books have appeared.

When wading through such references, it's important to keep your greatest need in mind, whether it's writing an effective resume, interviewing for a new position, or coping with an unreasonable boss. Look for resources that provide thorough, constructive advice on how to solve your most pressing problem quickly.

If creating powerful resumes and letters is your prime concern, then this book is such a resource. Loretta Foxman has compiled numerous examples of chronological, functional, and combination resumes, as well as an array of letters you can use as models when sitting down at your computer keyboard. Loretta's accompanying advice is top-notch, making this a career book that will continue to help readers long after most other bookstore guides are gone.

Tony Lee
Editor
National Business
Employment Weekly
Princeton, N.J.

ACKNOWLEDGMENTS

I wish to express my gratitude first and foremost to **Andrea Faugerstrom** for her diligence, patience, and hard work in helping me to complete this manuscript.

In addition, I would like to thank the principals and staff of Outplacement International, Inc. (OI) for their support, resources, and guidance. I have gathered their wisdom from over eighty offices—from Boston, Buffalo, Cincinnati, Cleveland, Dallas, Denver, Detroit, Ft. Lauderdale, Grand Rapids, Hartford, Irvine, London, Los Angeles, Louisville, Minneapolis, New York City, Paramus, Phoenix, Portland, San Francisco, San Jose, San Juan, Toronto, Tucson, and Washington, D.C., to name a few!—to bring together the best information available. I would like to extend special thanks to:

Steve Cuthrell & John Szymczak
OI/Cuthrell Szymczak
Buffalo, New York

William E. Snow, Ph.D.
OI/OPCI
Cleveland, Ohio

Karl B. Shinn
OI/The Curtiss Group
Ft. Lauderdale, Florida

Robert M. Donaldson
OI/Executive Career Services
Irvine, California

Jim Chapel
OI/Chapel Stowell
Lake Oswego, Oregon

John Hall
OI/KPMG Peat Marwick Stevenson & Kellogg
London, England

Gerald McGuire
OI/The McGuire Group
Los Angeles, California

Phillip Ronniger
OI/Ronniger
Louisville, Kentucky

F. Craig Barber
OI/Minnesota
Minneapolis, Minnesota

Madeline and Robert Swain
OI/Swain & Swain
New York, New York

Mark Nelson
OI/Nelson-Harper & Associates
Phoenix, Arizona

Sharon Gadberry, Ph.D.
OI/The Transitions Management Group
San Francisco, California

Barry Willis
OI/KPMG Peat Marwick Stevenson & Kellogg
Toronto, Ontario, Canada

And *all* the staff at
OI/Cambridge Human Resource Group
Chicago, Illinois

INTRODUCTION

So you're looking for a job . . . but you don't want just any job. You want a *career-building* job, one that uses your special talents and abilities, that meets your individual needs, and that will open the door to future opportunities. One of the most important things you can do to facilitate your search for this kind of career-building job is to develop a good resume. This significant marketing tool has the power to make a potential employer either want to meet you or want to toss your resume into the circular file. Trying to build your career without a good resume is like trying to build a house without a hammer and nails—it might be possible, but it's much more difficult!

This manual is designed as a workbook and guide to help you develop your own resume. It will help you think through the rationale behind writing your resume so you can communicate your unique skills and aspirations in the most effective way. Further, it will help you understand how to use your resume to enable you to achieve your overall career goals.

The workbook is divided into seven sections that outline the career-building process:

  I Blueprint for Success: Your Career Plan (Overview and Perspective)

 II Surveying Your Assets: Career Assessment (Skills and Accomplishments)

III Laying the Foundation: Your Career Goals (Goal Setting)

IV Hammering Out the Best of You: Your Resume (Complete Guide)

 V Tools of the Trade: Letters, Letters, Letters! (Seven Types of Letters)

VI Managing the Project: Strategies and Resources (What, Where, and How)

VII Model Marketing Tools: Samples (Proven Resumes and Letters)

HOW TO USE THIS WORKBOOK

STEP 1 Read the workbook thoroughly from cover to cover.

STEP 2 Complete Skills and Accomplishments Inventories.

STEP 3 Fill out Goals Definition and Job Goals Worksheets.

STEP 4 Prepare Pre-Resume Worksheet using:
- Your first and second choice job goals
- Accomplishments Inventory
- Skills Inventory
- Action-Oriented Word List
- Sample Accomplishments/Resumes as guides (if needed)

STEP 5 Go back and review this Pre-Resume Worksheet (the first draft of your resume).
- Be sure you have used verbs to define each accomplishment. The Action-Oriented Word List will help you think of even more action words.
- Be sure you have quantified each accomplishment whenever possible with numbers, percentages, dollars, etc.

STEP 6 Follow guidelines on putting together and printing your final resume.

STEP 7 Immediately begin keeping a log of all the resumes you distribute.

STEP 8 Refer back to each section as a review each time you begin a new job search activity. For example, before answering advertisements, reread that section of the workbook to refresh your memory of the best strategy to use.

STEP 9 Approach your job search energetically and with confidence. Combine the knowledge you have gained from the workbook about yourself and about the job search process with a positive and persevering attitude and you are bound for success!

Blueprint for Success: Your Career Plan

The problem job hunters really face is that they must impose on themselves those small disciplines that make large successes possible.

Steve Cuthrell and John Szymczak
OI*/Cuthrell Szymczak, Inc.
Buffalo, New York

It is true that when starting a job search, most individuals begin with and spend most of their time preparing their resume. As I mentioned in the introduction, the resume is a very important tool for the successful culmination of your job search. However, as important as it is, your resume by itself is not going to get you a job. Let's look at an overview of the steps in this Career Plan in order to put the resume into its proper perspective within your plan.

Each item preceded by an asterisk (*) is discussed in this workbook.

Step I: Commitment and Responsibility

* You must take charge of the job hunt.
* You must take responsibility for making the commitment to put in the time and energy needed.
* You must plan, organize, and control your career plan.
* You must make sure you follow through on each step in your job search effort.

Step II: Career Assessment

* You must interview yourself and find out:
  —What you like
  —What you dislike
  —What you value
  —What interests you
* —What you have accomplished (strengths)
* —What your skills are (strengths)
* —What your weaknesses are

Step III: Establish Career Goals and Objectives (immediate and long range)

* You must define your goals in written form before you begin writing your resume.
* If you are not sure of your goals, write the nearest general direction in which you believe your goals lie.
* Without this written focus and definition of your career objective, it will be difficult to develop an outstanding resume.

Step IV: Marketing Tools: The Resume, the Cover Letter, and the Broadcast Letter

* Write the resume that best sells you to a potential employer.
* Never send out a resume without a cover letter.
* In some instances, a broadcast letter should be used instead of a resume or cover letter.

Step V: Market Strategy

* You must develop and build a contact network. (We begin contact development in this book.)
* Develop a target organization list with the name of each person with the power to hire you. (We will begin research in this book.)

Step VI: Interviewing Skills Development

You must learn how to prepare for the interview:
—Appearance
—Researching the organization
—Researching the decision maker

You must learn how to ask significant questions.

You must learn how to answer the questions you could be asked in an interview

You must practice, practice, practice.

*An Outplacement International Company.

Step VII: Thank-You Letter

*   Write a thank-you letter to express appreciation to:
    —Your contacts
    —Your references
    —The interviewer
    This letter will set you apart from the herd, and hence make a significant impact on your job search.

Step VIII: Salary Negotiation

You must learn how to negotiate the best salary package for you.

Try to avoid mentioning your present salary or salary requirements to prospective employers before an offer has been made. Let the employer throw out the first figure to start the negotiation. When dealing with executive recruiters, however, be up-front about your salary requirements.

Step IX: Records

*   Keep a log of all resumes you send. Include date and follow-up (use Resume Log on pp. 34–35).

▐▌ Surveying Your Real Assets: Career Assessment

SKILLS

Who are you? Do you know what you are good at? what interests you? what motivates you? what trips you up? what you value most in a job? Whether you are just entering the job market, are making a career change, or are well into a successful career, it will pay for you to take the time to reevaluate yourself, your abilities, and accomplishments. First, a greater self-awareness will help you establish meaningful and realistic career goals. In addition, the better you know your strengths and abilities, interests and values, the better you can communicate them to your prospective employers.

In this section we will focus on assessing your skills and accomplishments, since knowledge of these areas is crucial to building an effective resume. The exercises that follow will explore what you have to bring to the workplace, the skills and abilities you will be trying to sell to your prospective employers; in the process you may remember some you had forgotten about. You may also find you have some weak areas that you would like to develop. Whatever you discover, your aim at this stage should be constructive and honest self-appraisal.

Surveying your values, likes, and dislikes is also important. While we will not address this phase of assessment in the workbook, be sure to do it on your own. There are many books on the market that can stimulate your thinking in this area. If you are interested in more comprehensive self-evaluation, you may want to contact a good career counselor who can administer and interpret a variety of career profiles for you. (See the Suggested Reading Section in the Appendix on page 115 for more information on available resources.)

SKILLS INVENTORY

INSTRUCTIONS:

The purpose of this activity is to discover your level of ability in each skill.

Step 1: *Self Evaluation*

Rate your skills using the following key:

S = Superior
A = Acceptable
N = Needs development
NA = Not applicable

Enter the appropriate letter in the LEVEL column below. If you have a specialized ability within a category, include it at the end of the list. For example, if you are in advertising, you may want to include more specific art skills on the Creative Abilities list, such as concept development.

CREATIVE ABILITIES

ABILITY	LEVEL
Composing	_____
Creativity	_____
Design	_____
Drawing	_____
Inventing	_____
Performing	_____
Resourcefulness	_____
Writing	_____
Other:	_____
_____	_____

COMMUNICATION/MANAGEMENT ABILITIES

ABILITY	LEVEL
Coordinating	_____
Diplomacy	_____
Directing	_____
Facilitating Discussion	_____
Foreign Language	_____
Leading	_____
Listening	_____
Managing	_____
Mediating	_____
Motivating	_____
Negotiating	_____
Persuading	_____
Presenting	_____
Promoting	_____
Public Speaking	_____
Selling	_____
Supervising	_____
Teaching	_____
Training	_____
Writing	_____
Other:	_____
_____	_____

INTELLECTUAL ABILITIES

ABILITY	LEVEL
Analysis	_____
Bookkeeping	_____
Decision Making	_____
Editing	_____
Evaluating	_____
Observing	_____
Organizing	_____
Planning	_____
Problem Solving	_____
Program Development	_____
Policy Formulation	_____
Research	_____
Scheduling	_____
Studying	_____
Troubleshooting	_____
Other:	_____
_____	_____

TECHNICAL ABILITIES

ABILITY	LEVEL
Accounting	_____
Carpentry	_____
Computer Programming	_____
Construction	_____
Database Management	_____
Drafting	_____
Electronics	_____
Repair/Maintenance	_____
Typing	_____
Word Processing	_____
Other:	_____
_____	_____

SKILLS INVENTORY

Step 2: *Peer Evaluation*

Ask someone who knows you well professionally (a boss, colleague or subordinate) to rate your skills using the same key:

S = Superior
A = Acceptable
N = Needs development
NA = Not applicable

Enter the appropriate letter in the LEVEL column below. If you wrote in additional skills on the first worksheet, include them here as well.

CREATIVE ABILITIES

ABILITY	LEVEL
Composing	_____
Creativity	_____
Design	_____
Drawing	_____
Inventing	_____
Performing	_____
Resourcefulness	_____
Writing	_____
Other:	_____
_____	_____

COMMUNICATION/MANAGEMENT ABILITIES

ABILITY	LEVEL
Coordinating	_____
Diplomacy	_____
Directing	_____
Facilitating Discussion	_____
Foreign Language	_____
Leading	_____
Listening	_____
Managing	_____
Mediating	_____
Motivating	_____
Negotiating	_____
Persuading	_____
Presenting	_____
Promoting	_____
Public Speaking	_____
Selling	_____
Supervising	_____
Teaching	_____
Training	_____
Writing	_____
Other:	_____
_____	_____

INTELLECTUAL ABILITIES

ABILITY	LEVEL
Analysis	_____
Bookkeeping	_____
Decision Making	_____
Editing	_____
Evaluating	_____
Observing	_____
Organizing	_____
Planning	_____
Problem Solving	_____
Program Development	_____
Policy Formulation	_____
Research	_____
Scheduling	_____
Studying	_____
Troubleshooting	_____
Other:	_____
_____	_____

TECHNICAL ABILITIES

ABILITY	LEVEL
Accounting	_____
Carpentry	_____
Computer Programming	_____
Construction	_____
Database Management	_____
Drafting	_____
Electronics	_____
Repair/Maintenance	_____
Typing	_____
Word Processing	_____
Other:	_____
_____	_____

SKILLS INVENTORY

Step 3: *Analysis*

List in the appropriate column below those skills that <u>both</u> you and your evaluator marked **Superior** (S), those that <u>both</u> of you marked **Needs Development** (N), and those that you rated differently.

Discuss with your evaluator the skills which you rated differently and decide together on a final rating. Circle those items you agree should be rated **Superior** (S) and underline those you agree **Need Development** (N).

This should give you a clearer picture of your strengths and weaknesses.

Superior	Needs Development	Disagree
1.	1.	1.
2.	2.	2.
3.	3.	3.
4.	4.	4.
5.	5.	5.
6.	6.	6.
7.	7.	7.
8.	8.	8.
9.	9.	9.
10.	10.	10.
11.	11.	11.
12.	12.	12.
13.	13.	13.
14.	14.	14.
15.	15.	15.

ACCOMPLISHMENTS

Each entry must prove your claims to an interviewer. We recommend a series of detailed vignettes that highlight your greatest successes and give a good idea of your strengths and experiences.

Madeline Swain and Robert Swain
OI/Swain & Swain
New York, New York

DEFINITION

An accomplishment is an activity in which you have done a *good* job, feel a sense of *pride* in having done it, and enjoyed doing it. Daniel Webster tells us an accomplishment is "work completed," "done successfully," "achievement."

PURPOSE

Although your potential employer will want to know about titles and responsibilities, the decision to hire you will be based on your accomplishments:

- Can you increase profits? or
- Can you deliver services or increase efficiency?

You will need a list of your accomplishments as a constant reference throughout your job search.

1. It is the basis for all communication (both written and oral).
2. It will prepare you for each interview (as you consistently refer to and then apply these accomplishments to the particular job interview).

Directions for Developing the Accomplishments Inventory:

- Complete both Worksheets I and II. These lists should cover your entire career (paid and nonpaid).
- Be concise and specific. (These phrases should be written so that they can be used "as is" in all written communication.)
- Use the Action-Oriented Word List (see page 13) to help demonstrate what you have actually accomplished.
- Use numbers to substantiate your results (contributions):
  NO: Responsible for significant increase in sales volume.
  YES: Increases annual sales volume by $270,000.
- If you cannot readily find the needed statistics, make an educated guess, keeping what is actual as your objective.
- Avoid unnecessary words.

ACTION-ORIENTED WORDS

Accelerated	Expanded	Recommended
Achieved	Formulated	Reduced
Administered	Generated	Reorganized
Analyzed	Headed	Researched
Built	Implemented	Set Up
Conceived	Improved	Simplified
Conducted	Innovated	Sold
Contracted	Installed	Solved
Converted	Invented	Streamlined
Created	Launched	Strengthened
Cut	Led	Succeeded
Delivered	Maintained	Supervised
Designed	Managed	Supported
Developed	Negotiated	Trained
Devised	Operated	Translated
Directed	Organized	Trimmed
Doubled	Performed	Tripled
Drafted	Planned	Uncovered
Edited	Prepared	Unified
Eliminated	Produced	Unraveled
Established	Programmed	Widened
Evaluated	Promoted	Won
Exhibited	Provided	Wrote

ACCOMPLISHMENTS INVENTORY WORKSHEET LIST I (Paid)

For each position you have held, identify your accomplishments. Include those accomplishments completed under your supervision by a subordinate(s).

As you develop the list, keep this criterion in mind:
- What was accomplished because you were there?
- Or, had you not been present, what would not have been accomplished?

Dates:
Title:
Company:
Accomplishments:

ACCOMPLISHMENTS INVENTORY WORKSHEET LIST I (Paid)

Dates:
Title:
Company:
Accomplishments:

Dates:
Title:
Company:
Accomplishments:

ACCOMPLISHMENTS INVENTORY WORKSHEET LIST II (Non Paid)
Organization Membership

List all groups of which you have been a member in the past or present. Include civic, social, cultural and professional.

Group:
Responsibility:
Accomplishments:

Group:
Responsibility:
Accomplishments:

III Laying the Foundation: Your Career Goals

The reader should be able to visualize what you expect to be doing from the contents of your resume. If you can't visualize it, chances are that no one else will be able to.

Sharon Gadberry, Ph.D.
OI/Transition Management Group
San Francisco, California

GOALS DEFINITION

How to Set Job/Career Objectives

A clear understanding of where you want to go is critical to a successful resume and ultimately to a successful job search. Your first task is to decide where you are going. The more specific you are about your destination, the easier it will be for your resume to take you there. Furthermore, if your resume is overly general, the strength of your credentials and your candidacy is diminished.

INSTRUCTIONS

1. Write a paragraph describing each of your career goals. If you have only one, that's fine. Rank them in order of importance to you and then write your top three career objectives (if you have three) in the Goals Definition Worksheet.

2. Be sure to include the following information:

   - Title and description
   - Field
   - Function
   - Company size
   - Responsibilities
   - If you wish to manage others, identify how many
   - Career growth potential
   - Environment (even if it seems unimportant, like a view from your office window)
   - Anything else that is important to you

3. Be concise and specific.

GOALS DEFINITION WORKSHEET

POSITION OBJECTIVE   Rank:

Title/Description

Field

Function

Company Size

Responsibilities

# of Subordinates

Growth Potential

Environment

Other

POSITION OBJECTIVE   Rank:

Title/Description

Field

Function

Company Size

Responsibilities

# of Subordinates

Growth Potential

Environment

Other

POSITION OBJECTIVE   Rank:

Title/Description

Field

Function

Company Size

Responsibilities

# of Subordinates

Growth Potential

Environment

Other

JOB GOALS - WORKSHEET I

"If your resume is too general, you won't be an obvious choice for any job."

Barry Willis
OI/KPMG Peat Marwick Stevenson & Kellogg
Toronto, Canada

1. Choose the two positions you ranked highest on the Goals Definition Worksheet.
2. Use the results of the Skills Inventory to fill in the My Skills column.

JOB TITLE #1 _____

SKILLS REQUIRED:	MY SKILLS:
1.	1.
2.	2.
3.	3.
4.	4.
5.	5.
6.	6.
7.	7.
8.	8.
9.	9.
10.	10.

JOB TITLE #2 _____

SKILLS REQUIRED:	MY SKILLS:
1.	1.
2.	2.
3.	3.
4.	4.
5.	5.
6.	6.
7.	7.
8.	8.
9.	9.
10.	10.

JOB GOALS   WORKSHEET II

Write your #1 job title from Job Goals Worksheet I

Job Goal (immediate)	**What Do I Need to Get There?**
The job I want most within 6 months is:	Means or Steps
	1.
	2.
	3.
	4.
	5.

Job Goal (midrange)	**What Do I Need to Get There?**
The job I want in 2 years is:	Means or Steps
	1.
	2.
	3.
	4.
	5.

Job Goal (long-range)	**What Do I Need to Get There?**
The job I want in 10 years is:	1.
	2.
	3.
	4.
	5.

IV Hammering Out the Best of You: Your Resume

WHAT IS A RESUME?

The resume (called the CV or curriculum vitae in the United Kingdom and Europe) is a snapshot of your professional career in words. It is an outline of the highlights of your professional accomplishments. A prospective employer is interested in one thing—*profits*. Therefore, as you write your resume, answer these two questions:

1. What have you done?
2. Does your resume demonstrate how you can improve services and/or profits?

> *Employers are paying for "results." You may think they love you, but be assured, they only love you as long as you are getting results.*
> Robert M. Donaldson
> OI/Executive Career Services
> Irvine, California

PURPOSE

The main reason for developing a resume is for *you*.

- To establish a written inventory of your strengths and accomplishments.
- To substantiate your confidence in yourself.
- To help you review your strengths before an interview for a particular position (a memory jogger).
- To help you project an "I can do this job" attitude *during* the interview.
- And, of course, to help you get the interview!

A WORD ABOUT STYLE

Make the style of your resume work for you. Your background will be enhanced by the *clarity* of vision expressed (where you want to go) and the *power* of the action-oriented words. Furthermore, your credibility will be reinforced by using the vocabulary and writing style typical of the field and position you are targeting.

Tell the Truth

Be truthful; use these words to hit home, not to embellish. Readers are smarter now. They see too many coached resumes, so they have good reason to be suspect of "expanding" accomplishments. Be mindful of the reader's sensitivity to this oversell approach.

The Word "I"

A resume that reads like an autobiography is inappropriate for most situations. Using an "I did this and I did that" style is poor form and poor taste. We recommend you begin each sentence with an action verb in the past tense (even if you are presently still doing it).

Consistency

Use the same writing style throughout the resume. Use either full sentences or incomplete sentences, never both.

Current Resume

Never send off a resume that has your most recent experience typed onto an old copy of your resume! Nor would we recommend just tacking on your most recent experience before retyping. Times have changed since your last resume and so have you. So, before reusing old material, make sure it will work for you with your current objectives and the current business climate.

> *People keep changing their cars, their houses, their wardrobes, but not their resumes. It is not unusual for someone to have a very old resume which they have tried to update by merely adding*

the last few job changes. The result is an improper and weak resume.

Gerald McGuire
OI/The McGuire Group
Los Angeles, California

You, the Author of the Resume

You should have a major stake in the writing of your resume. It should have your "signature" on it. If you do decide to go for help, a good career counselor or resume service can assist you in pulling it together. Their objectivity and knowledge of strategy and the workplace can make a significant difference.

A word of caution: Before you choose an advisor, do your homework. Ask for and check out thoroughly:

1. References (What kinds of people have they helped? Are they people like you?)
2. *Their* resume (Do they have the business experience and the credentials needed to be effective?)
3. Do they know firsthand how hiring decisions are made?
4. Is your background going to be plugged into a canned format or will they tailor the resume to your needs and objectives?

WHAT SHOULD IT CONTAIN?

Look at your resume as your advertising piece. Be smart, look at the way advertising is written: short, to the point and focused on what the advertiser believes are your needs and how his product can get those results.

Robert Donaldson
OI/Executive Career Service
Irvine, California

Instructions

You will need to research the following information about yourself.

- Personal Information
- Education
- Qualifications (Skills and Abilities)
- Experience (Employment History)
- Professional Activities
- Community Activities
- Honors and Awards
- Military Experience (if applicable)
- References

Position Objective

Leave this subject for your cover letter. Write your objective(s) here only to keep your thoughts goal-oriented. It should not be included in the resume itself, because it could limit the use of your resume or the options otherwise available to you.

Personal Information

Leave out anything that might be misconstrued, such as names and ages of children, references to height, weight, health, race, religious affiliation, or family background. Include:

Name
Address
Telephone number(s)

You may consider including other personal information, *if that information is likely to be strongly associated with your potential success*. For example, sales executives tend to look favorably upon hiring men who are tall. So, if you fall in that category and are looking for a sales position, it could be to your advantage to include your height and weight. However, if there is *any* question about the usefulness of the information, leave it out.

In the United Kingdom and Canada (*not* in the United States), other personal data, such as date of birth, marital status, and number of children can be added (optional) at the end of the resume under "Personal." Barry Willis of OI/KPMG Peat Marwick Stevenson & Kellogg in Toronto recommends you include it only if it adds value.

Education

This information can be placed near the beginning of your resume or at the end, depending on the power of your particular educational credentials. If you have no college degree, put education at the end (or leave if off the resume entirely). Similarly, if your college/graduate education is not directly related to the field or industry you have targeted, put it at the end of your resume. On the other hand, if you have just recently graduated from college, have just earned a graduate/postgraduate degree that is directly applicable to your field of interest, or if you have a degree from a top school (e.g., Stanford University), you will probably want to highlight that degree by placing it near the top of your resume.

Qualifications (Career Summary)

This introductory segment is a key piece of the resume. The reader can see a snapshot of the professional you in an instant. The "Qualifications Summary" is not usually about your personal characteristics. It can include skills, capabilities, significant achievements, breadth and depth of experience. It can be a listing or a narrative. Brevity (no more than seventy words) is important. If you use a narrative style, aim for three to five sentences maximum.

Experience (Employment History)

This includes paid and nonpaid experience. Use the Action-Oriented Word List on page 14 to develop and write your inventory of accomplishments. It is often helpful to include a very brief description of the organizations where you worked in addition to your accomplishments there. This is especially true for smaller and less well known companies. The format you use depends on your particular background. (See the section entitled: What Type of Format Is Best for You? page 24)

Professional Activities

These include papers or presentations, organizations (as member, officer, etc.), publications, committees, conferences or seminars (as attender or worker).

Community Activities

If the activity is related or appropriate to your career objective, include it. For example:

Northern Area Senior Center, Healthcare Committee, chaired and wrote a study.

This activity is particularly appropriate for your resume if your objective is in the health field or requires a writing skill.

Honors and Awards

Include these if timely or appropriate. If you have been out of college for twenty years, some of your college awards may be too old to mention. However, if the award related specifically to your field or job objective or is prestigious in nature, you may want to include it.

Interests (Optional)

Though a listing of interests is not a mandatory addition to the resume, it can be an enhancement. Depending on the particular interest, it could be a starting point for having something in common with the reader, or it could be a value-added dimension. *Caution:* Do not include an interest that could prejudice the reader against you. Think carefully about the statement you are making about yourself by including the interest and how the reader might respond. For example, you may be a champion cross-stitcher, but if you are a woman trying to break into a male-dominated field, don't even think about including it in your resume! In addition, it is generally best not to mention involvement with religious, political, or other potentially controversial groups unless they directly relate to the job you want.

> *Interests are optional, but can be productive in our experience.*
>> John Hall
>> OI/KPMG Peat Marwick Stevenson & Kellogg
>> London, England

Military Experience

Include whether you were an officer or enlisted. Remember to include your achievements. If you have no military experience, naturally this heading won't be necessary.

References

The accepted practice is *not* to mention the subject of references on the resume. When asked, be prepared to offer the names, addresses and phone numbers of three people who know you professionally and can vouch for your competence. Of course, before giving out anyone's name, be sure you have asked their permission first. For higher level candidates you may be asked for more than three references.

What Not to Include

1. Names and ages of children
2. Photographs
3. Position desired (this belongs in the cover letter)
4. Irrelevant words and phrases
5. Salary
6. Reasons for job change
7. Unnecessary references to height, weight, health, race, religious affiliation, or family background.

WHAT TYPE OF FORMAT IS BEST FOR YOU?

There are several types of resumes. For our purposes we will discuss the three most universally appropriate:

- Chronological
- Functional
- Combination

Chronological

This format is a listing of all jobs in reverse order beginning with the most recent. It is the most common and is the easiest for the reader to scan (he or she is probably most familiar with this type). If you have had no employment gaps and if you have held successively more responsible positions, this format will clearly show your continuous and upward career growth.

Functional

The emphasis of this format is on experience, skills, and accomplishments. Major functions or skills are listed with specific accomplishments centered below each topic (see sample functional resume on page 89). The focus on skills and accomplishments and the ability to hide any voids in one's previous employment are the advantages of the functional resume.

The very general picture of one's work experience and the lack of specific data are strong disadvantages, however. *This is the least preferred resume. Use it only when you have no other choice.*

Combination

This type of resume is a mixture of both the *chronological* and the *functional*. In one sense, it is the most complete resume, because it combines the flexibility of the functional resume with the specifics of the chronological. Since it is less familiar than the chronological, however, it can be more difficult for the reader to follow this format. For people with unconventional work histories, this format is preferred over the functional.

A Last Word on Format

The chronological resume is still the format most readers prefer. Use it whenever possible. In addition, any format that does not include a career history is not acceptable in the United Kingdom.

HOW TO HANDLE PROBLEMS UNIQUE TO YOUR BACKGROUND

Advanced in Age

Things are changing; the workforce is growing older. Advanced in age, though potentially a problem, is not the issue it once was. Thus, we recommend showing early work experience, summarizing multiple years in one paragraph, if necessary. If you think your age could be a problem for you, you can leave out the first ten or more years on your resume; that is, beginning your work experience section in 1968 instead of 1958. Another strategy is to send a broadcast letter only (without a resume).

You Are Coming Out of the Military, Government Service, or Education to Private Industry

Identify your accomplishments as they would relate to the position(s) and industry(ies) you are pursuing. Avoid jargon that is related to the situation you are leaving.

You Have Changed Jobs Frequently

One good way to handle this issue is to lump some of your positions together under one time span and then list your accomplishments underneath. For example:

1985 to 1992	**PUTNEY, INC., Denver, Colorado** *Manager Accounting* **BANK NORTH AMERICA, Aurora, Colorado** *Senior Accountant* **EVERGREEN LIFE INSURANCE CO., Aurora, Colorado** *General Accountant*

- **Monitored formal forecasting and budget system for department; increased financial accountability resulted in reducing spending by $15,000.**

- **Set up standard cost accounting and production system at branch location; visited and evaluated to ensure effective implementation.**
- **Authored and implemented variable selling expense procedures to improve control and expense processing. Reduced man hours by 10 hours per month.**

Another way to handle a "frequent job change" history is to send a letter without a resume, highlighting selected portions of your resume.

A third strategy is to briefly explain the frequent job changes in the cover letter. If you follow this strategy, be sure to cast the experience in a positive light.

Your Experience Does Not Directly Relate to Your Targeted Position

Use terminology that relates to your career objective rather than to your last experience. Select and also rewrite your accomplishments to better relate to your targeted objective. If the industry you come from could lead the reader in the wrong direction, camouflage it by describing the industry in more general terms. For example, instead of "Coroon and Black, a major insurance brokerage firm" you could say, "Coroon and Black, a leading financial organization" or "a major service firm."

You Lack Necessary Experience in Your Targeted Area

Use accomplishments that indicate you are person who possesses drive and a high degree of intelligence, which can compensate for your lack of specific experience. Any previous career and/or responsibility change should indicate that the change was successful.

You Have Gaps in Your Employment

Use the same strategy as explained above for frequent job changes.

HOW SHOULD IT LOOK?

When you think you have spent about as much time as needed on building an interview generating resume, you have only just begun. Continue to make refinements and adjustments. After all, your resume is part of your overall Strategic Marketing Plan.

Karl Shinn
OI/The Curtiss Group
Fort Lauderdale, Flordia

Paper

Use white bond (25 lb rag is recommended). We suggest that you stay away from color, including grey. If you really want to use colored paper, use ivory (off-white is fine). Generally, color is a sign that you want your resume to be noticed. It is not the resume but your actual accomplishments that will entice the reader. The choice of a color can become an overstatement.

Size

Always use the standard 8-1/2″ × 11″ paper (8-1/2″ × 11-5/8″ in the United Kingdom and Europe). Some experts recommend legal size or slightly smaller than standard as alternatives. However, we recommend you stay with the standard size, because if it is too big it is cumbersome, and if it is too small it could easily get lost.

Word Processing

It is of paramount importance that your resume be free of errors. Therefore, proofread the resume at least twice after the final draft. We recommend you have two others proofread this last draft as well. Use a word processor with a laser printer for a clear, clean copy. Typing your resume is passé. There are two major advantages to word processing. The first has to do with ease in making corrections, updates, and changes. Second, the ability to use typeset-like fonts is important. (Remember to use typestyles that are clear and businesslike rather than artsy.)

Duplication

Ideally, you should have your resume printed by a professional. The offset process is recommended because it presents a clean, clear copy for a small amount of money. Never use carbon copies. As a rule, we do not recommend photocopies. However, if you have an excellent (let me emphasize the word *excellent*) copier and you use heavyweight paper, photocopying is fine. The rule is, if you can tell it is a photocopy, it is not okay. We are talking about common sense here. Your resume will often be the first impression the reader gets of you.

Special Effects

Do not overuse underlining, capitalization, bold, and italics. These effects can be used to highlight important points. However, if overdone, they make the resume more difficult to read and to follow.

Spacing

For clarity, leave ample spacing at the top, the bottom, the sides, and in-between sections. This makes it easier for the reader to make notes in the margins, but most importantly, it makes it easier to read.

Name Change of Former Employer

Write the company's present name first, then the former name immediately following:

United Can Company, formerly known as Cutler Can, Inc.

Abbreviation

As a rule, spell out every word (including titles) unless the abbreviation is broadly understood and will make the resume easier to read. College degrees are typically abbreviated (with or without periods). For example, MBA or M.B.A. is universally understood and is much easier to read than Master of Business Administration. Other *very common* business abbreviations, such as P&L (profit and loss) are also acceptable.

Length

The general rule is that your resume must not exceed two pages. After writing all that you can possibly write, you must then condense it to one or two pages. However, if it is to your advantage to break this rule, you may want to do so. Some possible exceptions to this rule include the following:

1. Your industry requires only one page. For example, in the theater, an actor must have only one page, because his or her 8″ × 10″ glossy photograph must be glued to the back.
2. You live in an area (such as Canada) where two or three pages is readily accepted.
3. You are a very senior executive who has good reason to go over two pages. However, for 99 percent of the executive population, two pages works well (and is preferred in the U.S. job marketplace). One career expert had these words to say about the two-page limit:

In working with senior executives over six figures, we have had good success with more than two page resumes that are narrative in nature, clearly organized both by headings and graphics. to give a complete picture of the context and challenge in which the executive achieved his or her accomplishments. This makes for a more fruitful discussion during the hiring process.
William E. Snow, Ph.D.
OI/OPCI
Cleveland, Ohio

A Final Word about Breaking the Rules

All rules have exceptions; those discussed here are no different. Don't be afraid to break with convention if you feel it will be to your benefit. However, before you do we would suggest the following:

1. Be certain you have a very strong rationale for breaking the rule.
2. Run your idea past someone else who is able to judge what its potential impact might be.

PRE-RESUME WORKSHEET

Before you complete this worksheet, be sure you have completed your accomplishment list.

The Pre-Resume Worksheet was developed to help provide focus for the resume. It is a memory jogger and will form the basis for your final resume. At this stage, work on getting all the necessary information on paper without getting bogged down with wording or organization. Once you have completed this worksheet, you can fine-tune, reshape, and reorganize the material as needed until you have a well-crafted and effective final version.

Personal Information

Education (school, degree, year, GPA and school related honors, if appropriate.)

Qualifications (skills)

PRE-RESUME WORKSHEET (*continued*)

Experience/Employment History

(Paid and non-paid. Depending on the format you choose, you may find it helpful to cut and paste here directly from the Accomplishments Inventory Worksheet you have already completed.)

PRE-RESUME WORKSHEET (*continued*)

Experience/Employment History

PRE-RESUME WORKSHEET (*continued*)

Experience/Employment History

PRE-RESUME WORKSHEET (*continued*)

<u>Experience/Employment History</u>

PRE-RESUME WORKSHEET (*continued*)

Professional Activities

Community Activities

Honors and Awards

Military Experience

References

GENERAL GUIDELINES FOR DISTRIBUTION

Use the resume:

- After you have decided on a specific career objective. If you have two substantially different job objectives, you may want to use two different resumes.
- After you have researched and targeted organizations in which you are interested.
- After you find the name of the appropriate decision maker in the organization. This is the individual who is authorized to hire you. This person is generaly two levels above the position you are seeking.

Send your resume directly to the individual (by name and title) within the most appropriate department who is in a high enough position to hire you. As a rule, do not send your resume to the personnel department unless you seek a position in personnel.

When going to an interview, have extra copies of your resume on hand in case the interviewer asks for another copy or would like to circulate your resume to others. If the interview has been set up by an executive recruiter, the interviewer will not need a copy of your resume—the recruiter will have already given the employer a detailed dossier outlining your background and qualifications. Always follow any interview with a thank-you letter. Use the Resume Logs provided here to manage and keep track of your resume.

RESUME LOG

Company Name Address and Telephone Number	Individual's Name and Title	Date and Comments	Follow-Up Date and Directions

RESUME LOG

Company Name Address and Telephone Number	Individual's Name and Title	Date and Comments	Follow-Up Date and Directions

V Tools of the Trade: Letters, Letters, Letters!

A good cover letter will emphasize that you want the job and are eagerly awaiting an interview.

Jim Chapel
OI/Chapel-Stowell
Lake Oswego, Oregon

COVER LETTER

Purpose

A cover letter is a tool that accompanies a resume or application. The purpose is to provide additional information that is not on the resume or to show how your experiences and skills match those of a specific position.

Guidelines

- A cover letter should always accompany the resume.
- Target the letter to the person and company to which you are sending it.
- It should always be addressed to a specific individual (name and title), unless it is in response to a blind ad.
- One page on standard-size paper (8-1/2″ × 11″ or 8-1/2″ × 11-5/8″ in the United Kingdom and Europe) is recommended—error-free, of course!
- Show confidence in the contents of the letter; however, be careful not to sound pompous.
- Be positive—don't be apologetic or negative.
- Keep it brief—don't be too wordy or philosophical.

- Each cover letter should be typed or printed on a letter-quality printer, not photocopied.
- Don't say that you will call soon—just do it!

People don't want to be told that they will be contacted shortly. That is not to say you don't do it.

John Hall
OI/KPMG Peat Marwick Stevenson & Kellogg
London, England

Content

An effective cover letter should include the following, suggests Jim Chapel of OI/Chapel Stowell in Greater Portland, Oregon:

1. Return address and phone number(s)
2. Date
3. Potential Employer's name and address
4. Salutation
5. Introductory paragraph
6. Statement of purpose
7. Brief summary of qualifications
8. Request for response
9. Closing and signature

Your Name
Your Present Address
City, State, Zip
(Area Code) Telephone Number

Date

Name of Employer
Position/Title
Name of Organization or Company
Address
City, State Zip

Dear Ms. or Mr. Potential Employer:

Tell why you are writing. Name the position or job area in which you are interested. If this is a letter of inquiry, state clearly that you are writing for consideration should a position exist. If this is a letter of application, state how you heard of the opening.

Give a summary of your qualifications; you can reword or leave them as is from the actual resume. Mention what you have to offer that would be of greatest importance to the employer. State any related experience or training that relates to the particular job and/or company requirements.

The third paragraph should make a specific request for a personal interview. Also, refer the reader to your enclosed resume and/or application form.

Sincerely,

Your Name Typed

Enclosure(s)

Types of Cover Letters

Executive Recruiter Letter—In addition to the above, add current salary or last cash compensation and salary requirements, if different from last compensation.

Inquiry Letter—Say you are interested should a position opening exist, or (if appropriate) ask to be networked to others who may want to know of you.

Specific Opening Letter—Name the title (if you know it) and how you know about the position.

Follow-Up Letter—This is a good opportunity to refer to a particular capability or point that you didn't mention or

sufficiently emphasize during your telephone or face-to-face discussion.

Networking Letter—This letter is sent to a wide circle of people ranging from those you know very well to those you have never met. This letter needs great care and attention. You may prefer to handwrite a note to someone you know well on a personal basis, but usually it is typed. However, do not let this letter substitute for a face-to-face meeting.

Thank-You Letter—You *can't* overdo this one, so be generous with your letters and notes of appreciation. This is usually sent without a resume. It can also be used as a followup letter, containing any information that was requested or overlooked at the meeting.

BROADCAST LETTER

There are times when a resume and cover letter are not specific enough for a particular job goal. Or, the resume could contain information not relevant to your objective. You might wish to send a broadcast letter when answering a blind advertisement in order to protect the personal data on your resume. The broadcast letter is used in place of the resume.

Instructions

- Before writing the broadcast letter, it is important to have completed the accomplishments lists.
- This letter, like your resume, should contain objective measures of job success:

  Facilitated three national training and development conferences for over 350 professionals.

  Initiated real estate tax review reducing current taxes by $97,000 and prior year by $47,000.

- The accomplishments done by your subordinates belong to your own list of accomplishments, because they were done under your responsibility, accountability, and supervision.
- This letter should contain a succinct inventory of actual tasks you have accomplished and problems you have solved with supporting quantitative data.
- Begin with position title and follow with the appropriate accomplishments:

  As Manager of Inventory Control, I redesigned the computerbased inventory control system, increasing cash flow by $1 million.

  As Administrative Secretary, I instituted a new procedure for submitting departmental expense reports that reduced the average turnaround by two days.

- Your broadcast letter should pertain to the position you are seeking and the organization you are targeting. (See sample pp. 113–114.)

VI Managing the Project: Strategies and Resources

I am a firm believer in the power of each person's ability to manage their job hunt successfully. With the right resources, even rusty or entry level job hunters can search effectively in a tight market.

Tony Lee
Editor, *National Business Employment Weekly*

Where should you look for a job or a lead? The decision depends on your background. Most job searchers use a combination of the following:

- Contacts
- Advertisements
- Association Publications and Trade Journals
- Direct Mail
- Yellow Pages
- Chamber of Commerce
- College Placement Offices and Publications
- Employment Agencies
- Contingency Executive Recruiters
- Retainer Executive Recruiters
- Consulting Firms/Law Firms/CPA Firms
- Your State Government
- Federal Government
- State Employment Service
- Business Reference Books

CONTACTS: AN IMPORTANT TOOL

Contacts are an important resource for jobs, leads, and referrals. Statistics show that use of contacts is the most successful job-hunting tool. Some studies indicate that as many as 85 percent of successful job searches are due to contacts.

Whenever possible, you will want to meet your contacts for a personal interview. Having met face to face, they can best remember *you*. You are no longer just a piece of paper—a resume. There are four types of contacts:

- Personal friends
- Business associates (colleagues, subordinates, or superiors)

- Individuals who may need to be reminded how they know you
- Individuals others refer you to

Care and Feeding

Before you begin, remember the most important rule: If you are not considerate and thoughtful of this most valuable resource, the game is over. You need their help. Without it, the job search is harder and takes longer. Be thoughtful of their time. If you ask for a fifteen-minute meeting, get up and leave after fifteen minutes unless you are asked to stay longer. Be generous with your appreciation. Say "thank you" after someone helps you, even if it's over the telephone. One candidate sent flowers to his former boss who had gone to great lengths to help.

Contact List Instructions:

Brainstorm and list *all* the people you can think of who might be able to help you. Aim for an initial list of fifty names. After you complete this first draft, give each potential contact a rank of A, B, or C, with A being the most potentially helpful. Then divide this list into separate pages respectively marked A, B, and C.

The A's should be contacted first, because these are the contacts that are most likely to lead you to a job or another good contact. When you have exhausted the A's, go to the B's (second-best sources), and finally the C's (the "long shots"). While it makes sense to focus the bulk of your efforts on the A and B contacts, don't neglect contacting your C list. Even though they may be long shots, you never know who is actually going to help you until you contact them. You may find that one of your C list contacts is much more helpful than one of your A list contacts.

As your job search progresses, your contact list should continue to grow because of the continuous referrals you will get.

CONTACT LIST (Brainstorm)

CONTACT LIST (Brainstorm)

CONTACT LIST A (BEST BETS)

NAME	TELEPHONE #	DATE CONTACTED	COMMENTS	FOLLOW-UP DATE

CONTACT LIST B (SECOND BEST)

NAME	TELEPHONE #	DATE CONTACTED	COMMENTS	FOLLOW-UP DATE

CONTACT LIST C (LONG SHOTS)

NAME	TELEPHONE #	DATE CONTACTED	COMMENTS	FOLLOW-UP DATE

ADVERTISEMENTS

Newspaper advertisements are often the first place job seekers look for a job. However, you should not depend on ads as a major source of employment. Remember, you are competing with hundreds of job seekers who are reading the very same ad.

On the other hand, don't ignore job advertisements completely. By responding to newpaper ads you may be able to tap into the "hidden job market"—other jobs within the organization that are still in the minds of the managers and have not yet been fully conceptualized and written down for the human resource department to place an ad.

You should approach the ads intelligently and with a specific strategy in mind to get the job you want.

- Answer ads even though your background doesn't exactly match. The "perfect candidate" usually does not exist. Do not be deterred, even if the ad requires a degree you do not have, or some skill or experience you do not have.
- You may very well fill the requirements of a position that would report to the position advertised.
- You may fill a position not yet advertised by the personnel department.

If your qualifications don't exactly match the requirements in an ad, you could send a direct letter without mention of the ad to the appropriate departmental decision maker (see discussion of direct mail on p. 50). This way you do not have to respond to the requirements listed in the ad, and you may have a better chance of getting past the initial screeners.

At the beginning of your job search, go back three months and cut out all the ads closely related to the position you are seeking. Paste them to the Past Advertisement Worksheet on page 48. Some positions that are advertised only once or twice can take up to a year before a suitable candidate is found.

An additional approach is to go back a full year. Call or write to the companies that interest you. The individual who was hired may not have worked out. (Use the Past Advertisement Worksheet.)

After researching previous ads, concentrate on the present ads. Clip and paste them on the Present Advertisement Worksheet on page 49.

Blind Ads

An ad that does not identify the employer is called a blind ad. Responses are sent to a box number. Most box numbers can be used for several months.

- Advantage: Blind advertisements can be a good source, because fewer applicants respond to them.

- Disadvantage: One reason a company uses a blind ad is to maintain anonymity from their own employees as well as their competition. Since you do not know which company placed the ad, you could be sending your resume to your own boss (that is, if you are still employed).

Consequently, we do not recommend responding to blind ads if you are currently employed. However, some newspapers, such as the Wall Street Journal, will provide an intermediary service for employed job seekers. If you call the newspaper, they will supply the name of a newspaper staff member to whom you can send your resume and cover letter. If the unnamed company is your current employer, they will not forward your reply.

Newspapers

Newspapers are a major informational source for company and industry trends as well as potential job openings. Use present as well as back issues to help you with this research. Look for:

- Company relocations
- Company or product expansions
- Company earnings
- Management changes (new ideas and/or major expansion of personnel)
- Classified ads for company growth trends, salary information, and potential jobs.

Local Newspapers

Small city and community papers tend to focus on lower-level positions. If you are entry level, this could be just right. However, if you are looking for a higher-level position in a particular area, it can be helpful to scan the ads and business news in the local papers specific to your preferred location.

Major Newspapers

The following major newspapers have ads covering all of the United States. The Sunday edition contains ads that are geared to more senior-level or more highly-paid job openings. Choose and subscribe to the relevant Sunday edition of the newspapers identified below:

ATLANTA NEWSPAPERS
P.O. Box 4689
Atlanta, GA 30302
(404) 526-5151 or (800) 944-7363 ext. 5024

THE BOSTON GLOBE
135 Morrissey Boulevard
Boston, MA 02107
(617) 466-1818 or (800) 622-6631

CHICAGO TRIBUNE
435 North Michigan Avenue
Chicago, IL 60611
(800) 874-2863

CLEVELAND PLAIN DEALER
1801 Superior Avenue, N.E.
Cleveland, OH 44114
(216) 344-4600 or (800) 622-6631

THE DALLAS MORNING NEWS
P.O. Box 655237
508 Young Street
Dallas, TX 75265
(214) 745-8383 or (800) 431-0010

DENVER POST
P.O. Box 1709
Denver, CO 80201
(303) 832-3232 or (800) 543-5543

THE DETROIT NEWS & FREE PRESS
321 W. Lafayette Boulevard
Detroit, MI 48231
(313) 222-6500 or (800) 395-3300

THE HOUSTON CHRONICLE
801 Texas Avenue
Houston, TX 77002
(713) 220-7211 or (800) 735-3811

LOS ANGELES TIMES
Times Mirror Square
Los Angeles, CA 90053
(213) 626-2323 or (800) LA TIMES

MIAMI HERALD
One Herald Plaza
Miami, FL 33132
(305) 350-2000 or (800) 441-0444

MINNEAPOLIS STAR TRIBUNE
425 Portland Avenue
Minneapolis, MN 55488
(612) 673-4343 or (800) 827-8742

NEW YORK TIMES
P.O. Box 520
Palos Park, IL 60464-0520
(800) 448-8905—Hartford, CT;
(800) 631-2500—Remainder of U.S.

PHILADELPHIA INQUIRER
400 N. Broad Street
Philadelphia, PA 19101
(215) 854-4320

SAN FRANCISCO EXAMINER AND CHRONICLE
925 Mission Street
San Francisco, CA 94103
(415) 777-7000 or (800) 281-3200

WASHINGTON POST
1150 15th Street, N.W.
Washington, D.C. 20071
(202) 334-6100 or (800) 627-1150—DE, MD, NJ and WV;
(800) 446-4425—Remainder of U.S.

The Wall Street Journal is the best resource for middle and upper management openings. It is published in four regional editions: Western, Southwestern, Midwestern, and Eastern. You will find the largest selection of ads on Tuesday. Subscribe to the regional edition that most interests you:

THE WALL STREET JOURNAL
200 Burnett Road
Chicopee, MA 01020
(800) 628-9320

A second *Wall Street Journal* source is the *National Business Employment Weekly*. It is a compilation of the weekly *Wall Street Journal* regional want ads, and also contains excellent articles that can prove quite helpful to the job seeker. Also, there is a weekly calendar of events that lists job clubs, career workshops, and seminars nationwide, with over 500 listings each week. The *National Business Employment Weekly* is the only known source of its kind for job hunters seeking the support of others in the same situation. In addition to these weekly features, there is twice-a-month listing of:

- executive-level jobs in the nonprofit sector
- business opportunites with advice on starting a business, buying a franchise, and other entrepreneurial ventures

Some of the best career management advice is also available on-line through Dow Jones News/Retrieval. This service offers helpful articles on how to look for a job successfully and how to manage your career. You can access this information with your own computer modem (should you have one) or utilize the services at some public libraries.

To subscribe to the weekly newspaper, contact:

NATIONAL BUSINESS EMPLOYMENT WEEKLY
200 Burnett Road
Chicopee, MA 01020
Attn: Circulation Department
(800) JOB HUNT or (800) 628-9320

To subscribe to the Dow Jones News/Retrieval computer service, call (609) 452-1511.

Another national source of job opportunities is the *National Ad Search*. This newspaper compiles job ads from seventy-five city newspapers from around the country.

NATIONAL AD SEARCH
P.O. Box 2083
Milwaukee, WI 53201
(414) 351-1398 or (800) 992-2832

Association Publications and Trade Journals

Nearly every industry or profession has a trade association. Association magazines and newsletters often have classified listings of job opportunities. The potential assistance (information as well as contacts) of the membership lists is worth your consideration.

Trade associations often have *membership directories*, which are available to members. If you can gain access to a directory, you may be able to contact members by mail and/or telephone. Most associations also have job referral services that put job seekers in touch with employers.

The Encyclopedia of Associations, Gale Research, Inc., is the authoritative source in identifying the most appropriate associations for the position(s) you seek. This directory comes in three different versions: International, National (U.S.), and Regional, State, and Local. With over 22,000 organizations listed, the National version is your best bet for finding major professional organizations.

Another valuable resource is *National Trade and Professional Associations of the U.S.*, Columbia Books, Inc., containing over 6,000 listings, including labor unions, technical societies, trade associations, and more.

PAST ADVERTISEMENT WORKSHEET

Paste here	Date Sent Resume/or Other	Date/ follow-up

PRESENT ADVERTISEMENT WORKSHEET

Paste here	Date Sent Resume/or Other	Date/ follow-up

IS THE DIRECT MAIL METHOD FOR YOU?

Direct mail is one way to reach the unadvertised jobs in the "hidden job market" mentioned earlier. This method, when used correctly, can be effective. However, an important caution is needed here. Covering the sky with paper is the old way of job hunting. The new, more effective way is based on strategy. Be clear about *where* and *how many*:

- Use the research sources in the Business Reference Books list found on pages 51–52 to locate the target companies that interest you.
- Be sure to address your letter to the name and title of the individual you believe (through your research) to be the decision maker. For the name of the key individual, use the directories suggested in the Business Reference Books list. If possible, call the company and ask for the name and correct title of the executive. Better yet, use your contacts to identify the best "who" in the organization.
- The broadcast letter might be appropriate here. However, if your resume fits the position you are seeking in the particular organization, then a cover letter and resume can be effective.
- One sign of a derailed job search is too much paper on the streets. So if you do decide to use a mail campaign, do it sparingly and with a definite rationale for using this strategy. If direct mail is the only way into those companies, then use it. However, if it is at all possible to have a contact lend a hand, this is even better.

OTHER SOURCES

Yellow Pages

This is a good source for names locally as well as in other states. Upon request, your local telephone company can provide you with out-of-town directories.

Chamber of Commerce

Most states and major cities have a directory of business and industry published by the state or city Chamber of Commerce. These directories provide first-rate information when you are interested in a particular geographic location.

Overseas Chambers of Commerce, Foreign Embassies, and American Embassies

The following sources should prove helpful if your interest is in:

- An American company in a foreign country
- A foreign company with an American susidiary
- A foreign company overseas

Foreign Chambers of Commerce—Your local Chamber of Commerce should be able to help you locate the addresses of foreign Chambers of Commerce.

American Embassies—Addresses and persons to contact are listed in a publication entitled *Key Offices of Foreign Service Posts*. You can purchase this directory for a nominal fee through the Government Printing Office (GPO). You can contact the nearest regional GPO (located in most major cities) or the main GPO in Washington D.C. (202-783-3238).

Foreign Embassies and Consulates—If you are in a major city like Chicago, use the white pages of the telephone book to locate phone numbers and addresses of the foreign embassies and consulates you are interested in. If the country you are interested in does not have an embassy or consulate in your area, call Directory Assistance in Washington D.C. (202-555-1212) for foreign embassy listings.

Foreign Companies/U.S. Companies with Foreign Locations—Contact the World Trade Academy Press in New York City (212-697-4999) for a listing of special directories of international businesses. You may also consult the directories listed in the Business Reference Books—International Business Directories section of this book. See page 52.

College Placement Offices and Publications

Many college placement offices provide lists of job openings as well as a registration service to applicants. Try the college you attended as well as the colleges or universities in the area in which you are interested. Evaluate whether the services and publications of these placement offices can be of assistance to you.

Employment Agencies

There are three types of employment agencies: those that focus primarily on nonexempt (administrative, secretarial, and clerical) placement, those that focus on exempt (professional/managerial) placement, and those that do both. The firms that specialize in exempt placement generally deal with salaries that range from $20,000 to $120,000, with the majority of applicants at the lower half of that range. Firms that handle nonexempt candidates make placements mainly in the $12,000 to $30,000 range.

Employment agencies are usually licensed by the state. At one time, charging a fee to the applicant was a common practice. This is generally not the case anymore. However, there are still some who do accept such fees. Our recommendation is to avoid those who require a fee from you. There are more than enough good no-fee agencies.

To find employment agencies in your area, start by looking in your local yellow pages. They often advertise in the "want ads" section of the local newspaper as well. Employment agencies are oftentimes willing to meet you, according to Ray Stopa, Senior Consultant at Dunhill of

Chicago, Inc. "Call the agency and ask for the manager or an experienced counselor. Say you'll be in the area on Thursday and would like to come by for a few minutes to drop off your resume and meet that counselor. . . . I am always glad to put a face with paper."

Contingency Executive Recruiters

There seems to be some confusion in the marketplace over the difference between "contingency" and "retainer" executive recruiters. Both call themselves "executive search firms" and they are alike in that both are hired by an organization to search for a particular candidate with a specific background and experience. However, a few characteristics set contingency firms apart.

1. They are paid upon placement (after the individual begins work).
2. They often specialize in a specific industry or field, such as sales or finance.
3. Some will present your credentials to a prospective employer if they see you as an outstanding candidate.
4. Their assignments are mainly in the mid- to lower-level salary range. However, there is overlap and some assignments can go up to six figures.

Retainer Executive Recruiters

A retainer firm is hired by an organization and paid in advance, usually at the start of the search. All or part of the fee is paid up front, whether a candidate is found and hired or not. The retainer firm works on higher-level salaries only. Don't expect a retainer firm to:

1. Market you to a client
2. Meet with you for a courtesy meeting (although they may do so as a favor to someone they know and trust).
3. Get you a job, even if they give you a face-to-face courtesy meeting.

Both contingency and retainer firms have an allegiance to the company that pays their fee. Neither is the place for career counseling, so don't go there for career advice.

The most complete listing of retainer and contingency search firms in North America (now in its 21st edition) is *The Directory of Executive Recruiters* ($39.95 postpaid from Kennedy Publications, Templeton Road, Fitzwilliam, NH 03447; 1-800-531-0007). This resource profiles more than 2,300 firms in nearly 4,000 offices and identifies more than 5,000 search consultants. Kennedy Publications also provides mailing labels for targeted groups of search firms.

I think it is helpful to point out that retainer firms are unlikely to be of help to individuals—except on rare occasions for highly qualified people in the

$100,000—plus wage bracket. Contingency firms are much more likely to be willing to "market" an attractive candidate to their clients.

David Lord
Managing Editor
Executive Recruiter News

Consulting Firms/Law Firms/CPA Firms

Consultants and other professionals, such as corporate lawyers and CPA's, can be invaluable networking resources. Since they service many different organizations, their list of contacts and understanding of the marketplace is generally very broad and current.

If you can, start by asking a professional you know for referrals of others who deal with your field of interest. Otherwise, you can find information through your local Yellow Pages, Chamber of Commerce listing or a directory of professional firms at your local library. The following directories of consulting firms are rather extensive:

Consultants and Consulting Organizations Directory, Gale Research, Inc. This directory contains entires of over 16,000 firms, individuals, and organizations active in consulting.

The Directory of Management Consultants, Kennedy Publications, Templeton Road, Fitzwilliam, NH 03447-9989 (800-531-0007 or 603-585-6544). Profiles over 1500 management consulting firms.

BUSINESS REFERENCE BOOKS

This list is the key to your company research. Once you establish your position and industry objectives, you then need to find:

- A list of target companies
- The name and title of the person with the power to hire you

The following books will assist you with this important research. Your Business Reference Librarian can help you locate and use these sources as well as direct you to other resources that might be especially useful for your particular needs.

General Business Directories

Standard and Poor's Register of Corporations, Directors and Executives. New York: Standard and Poor's Corporation. Published annually.

This is one of the most comprehensive resources, with over 55,000 corporations listed in volume 1 and 70,000 biographies of directors and executives in volume 2. Each entry in volume 1 includes general information about the company (address, phone, number of employees, estimated sales, and more) along with the names and titles of key personnel. The biographies in volume 2 include home and principal business addresses, date and place of birth, fraternal organization memberships, and business affiliations.

Moody's Manuals. New York: Moody's Investors Service. Published annually.

Moody's Investors Service publishes several manuals with information on publically owned corporations. Areas covered include Bank and Finance, Industrial, International, Common Stocks, and Over-The-Counter Stocks. These manuals give extensive financial and statistical data on each company in addition to addresses and key personnel information.

Directory of Corporate Affiliations. Wilmette, IL: National Register Publishing Co. Published annually.

This directory documents "who owns whom" in the corporate world, listing 5,000 parent companies, 500 privately owned companies and approximately 45,000 domestic divisions, subsidiaries, joint ventures and affiliates. Each entry includes general information and key personnel of the parent company and all its divisions, plant locations, subsidiaries, etc.

Corporate 1000. New York: Monitor Publishing Co. Published quarterly.

For up-to-date information on the leading 1,000 public manufacturing, service, and utility companies, this source is very useful. Besides basic information on the company and key personnel, many entries also include direct phone numbers for each executive.

Macmillan Directory of Leading Private Companies. Wilmette, IL: National Register Publishing Co. Published annually.

This directory is an excellent resource for researching the 7,000 largest privately owned companies.

Hoover's Handbook of American Business. Austin, TX: The Reference Press, Inc. Published annually.

This relatively new resource profiles over 500 "major enterprises," including a mix of public, private, government, and nonprofit organizations. Each profile includes information on the nature of the enterprise, its history, key executives, products and services, and financial performance. The profiles are succinct but informative, offering some information (especially historical) that is not found in most other directories.

Thomas Register of American Manufacturers. New York: Thomas Publishing Co. Published annually.

Volumes 17 and 18 of this 25-volume directory contain profiles of 152,000 manufacturing firms. The rest of the volumes list product and brand/trade name information.

Who's Who in Finance and Industry. Glenview, IL: Macmillan, Inc. Published biennially in September of odd years.

This directory contains biographies of over 23,500 individuals, including personal, career and family data.

International Business Directories

Hoover's Handbook of World Business. Austin, TX: The Reference Press, Inc. Published annually.

This directory profiles major corporations based outside the United States. Like the *American Business* companion volume, the profiles include business descriptions and historical background along with significant statistical information. In addition to the corporate profiles, this volume also profiles major world regions and 61 different countries.

International Directory of Corporate Affiliations. Wilmette, IL: National Register Publishing Co. Published annually.

This directory lists "who owns whom" internationally in the same format as the national version described above.

International Corporate 1000. New York: Monitor Publishing Co. Published annually.

Organized like its national counterpart, this directory lists the leading 1000 corporations based outside of the United States.

Directory of Foreign Manufacturers in the U.S. Atlanta, GA: Business Press. Published irregularly—last edition 1990; next edition expected in 1993.

Contains information on over 4,800 U.S. manufacturing, mining, and petroleum companies and the 2,300+ firms abroad that own them.

Other Business Sources

Business Organizations, Agencies, and Publications Directory. Detroit, MI: Gale Research, Inc. Published biennially in even years.

This directory lists approximately 24,000 different business-related organizations and publications.

Business Periodicals Index. Bronx, NY: H.W. Wilson Co. Published monthly with annual compilation.

This is an annotated index of articles and book reviews from 345 business periodicals.

For More Information

Directory of Special Libraries and Information Centers. Detroit, MI: Gale Research, Inc. Published annually.

This directory is useful for finding specialized libraries in your area. Areas of specialization include business, government, law, computers, engineering, science, and health.

Directories in Print. Detroit, MI: Gale Research, Inc. Published annually.

With information on approximately 14,000 directories and professional rosters, this resource will help you find more specialized directories.

VII Model Marketing Tools: *Samples*

SAMPLE ACCOMPLISHMENTS

The key to an outstanding resume is to validate your previous successes. Your accomplishments best validate and demonstrate your potential contribution to a prospective employer. The following list of Sample Accomplishments will help you write your own regardless of whether you are:

- An executive or manager
- A professional
- A not for profit candidate
- A recent college graduate

Executive/Manager

- Recommended and implemented the consolidation of two departments that streamlined duplicate service and costs by $450,000.
- Reduced total defects per product unit by over 40 percent for two of the last five years, resulting in quality awards.

Professional

- As a Systems Analyst, conducted a major study culminating in a recommendation to upgrade mainframe computer, resulting in an ROI of 35 percent after two years.
- As Tax Attorney, managed aggressive, innovative tax planning and analysis for all corporate operations in federal, international, and state tax areas. Saved $850,000 annually.

Not for Profit

- Key participant in planning and implementing National Foundation for the Homeless annual fund-raiser. Generated corporate commitment totaling $6 million.
- As membership chairperson for the Illinois State United Way Board, recruited more new volunteers in two years than had been recorded in the agency's history.

Recent College Graduate

- As Program Chair of Alpha Phi social sorority, planned and implemented an annual function to raise money for Golden Age Senior Citizen Project. Resulted in dollar increase over previous year of $400.
- As a member of the Campus Organization Committee, developed new orientation program for freshmen and co-wrote an orientation manual.

SAMPLE RESUMES

The following resume samples are divided by format: chronological, combination and functional. You will find that the majority of our resume samples use the chronological format, since this is by far the most well accepted format. We have tried to include sample chronological resumes from a broad cross-section of functions and industries and have arranged them roughly in order of increasing experience and responsibility.

In order to illustrate acceptable versions of combination and functional resumes, we have included a few samples of those formats as well. However, we strongly discourage using the combination or functional formats unless you have a very compelling reason to do so.

You may find it helpful to peruse all of the sample resumes for ideas to use when writing your own resume—whether or not they are in the same format or match the position or industry you are targeting.

Chronological Resumes

DAVID R. GARCIA
429 East Winter Place
Flagstaff, AZ 86001
(602) 555-4321

EDUCATION

B.A., Native American Studies, **Northern Arizona University**, Flagstaff, AZ, 1992.

Key accomplishments:

- Award recipient of Lois Duncan Kellogg Grant for academic excellence, three time awardee: Spring 1989, Fall 1989, Spring 1990
- Maintained GPA of 3.5/3.75
- Enrolled in Honors program Spring 1989 through graduation.

WORK EXPERIENCE

1991-
Present

GREAT AMERICAN PAINT COMPANY, Flagstaff, AZ
<u>Sales/Inventory Clerk</u>

Reported to Store Manager. Worked part time in Flagstaff's major outlet/distributor. Liaison between three departments; maintained inventory; worked with retail and wholesale customers. Assisted in selecting and mixing chemical paint formulas.

Summer 1990
Summer 1991

CONEX INC., Chicago, IL
<u>Technician, Pest Control</u>

Was contacted long distance and requested to return for a second summer. Provided technical service for commercial and residential accounts. Worked as part of the service fleet. Entrusted with company car and cellular telephone. Responsible for maintaining all technical equipment. Participated in technical training and achieved proficiency quickly.

1987-1988
Summer 1988
Summer 1989

R. W. CARLSON, Glencoe, IL

A wholesale and retail paint and wallpaper outlet of high end product lines. Worked as team leader to provide customer satisfaction in all aspects of responsibilities. Key contributions included shipping/receiving, sales, stocking, ordering, inventory, hiring/training and field work.

OTHER INTERESTS

Camping, music and tennis.

JANET A. BARON

Current Address (until May 1992):
1423 Beacon Street, Apt. #4A
Boston, Massachusetts 02115
(617) 555-6888

Permanent Address:
2535 Rosemary Terrace
Deerfield, Illinois 60015
(708) 555-4793

EDUCATION

BOSTON UNIVERSITY, Boston, MA, Expected date of Graduation May 1992
B.A., Psychology. Major GPA: 3.8/4.0

RELATED COURSEWORK

Social Psychology	Organizational Behavior I & II	Marketing
Psychology of Gender	Statistics I, II & III	Publicity & Public Relations
Developmental Psychology	Research Methods I & II	Finance
Abnormal Psychology	Microeconomics	Financial Accounting

BUSINESS EXPERIENCE

Fall 1990   **INTERNSHIP, WELLINGTON TOWN COUNCIL**, London, England

- Researched and organized information on local organizations.
- Compiled and developed information for monthly newsletter.

Summer 1990   **GREAT ADVENTURES DAY CAMP**, Cambridge, MA
A summer day camp program for children

- Head Counselor. Planned and implemented events. Oversaw the work of four counselor aids. Helped plan all major camp activities.

Summer 1989   **CAMBRIDGE HUMAN RESOURCE GROUP, INC.**, Chicago, IL
A human resources consulting firm specializing in outplacement, assessment and organizational consulting.

- Provided administrative support for consultants and outplacement clients.

Summer 1988   **COOKIE DELITES**, Skokie, IL
A consumer food retail outlet.

- Participated in training for customer satisfaction at level required by corporation. Worked as part of sales team to support manager.

ACTIVITIES

Alpha Phi International Fraternity, Philanthropy Chairperson
College of Basic Studies, Peer Advisor
South Campus Student Government, Dorm Representative

SUSAN J. CECIL
1220 Cottonwood Drive
Aurora, CO 80018
(303) 555-6257

QUALIFICATIONS SUMMARY

Mechanical engineer with experience in plant engineering, equipment design and plant operations. Exposure to engine research. A hands-on professional with innovative ideas. Good ability to work with personnel at all levels.

EDUCATION

B.S., Mechanical Engineering, University of Illinois, Urbana, IL, 1992
Emphasis: Metal fabrication & machining, internal combustion engines

PROFESSIONAL HISTORY

Sept - May
1991 - 1992

TECHNOLOGY CENTER, University of Illinois, Urbana, IL

Research Assistant

- Designed laboratory equipment to measure the amount of cycle to cycle soot formation in diesel engines; teamed with German researcher from Siemens.

- Assisted with the installation of Caterpillar engine used in research.

- Researched laser doplar velocity measuring; designed experiment, coordinated data gathering and tabulated results.

Summers
1990, 1991

PANTLE STEEL, INC., Denver, CO
A manufacturer of seamless stainless steel tubing.

Summer Intern

- Reported to Plant Engineer; designed and drafted equipment modifications.

- Redesigned and installed conveyor clutch on annealing furnace; planned layout and directed relocation of 2" tube straightener.

- Designed automatic mandrel lubrication equipment; oversaw installation of 2" Pilger mill motors and lubrication line.

- Supervised five maintenance men and outside contractors during scheduled plant shutdown; contracted outside fabrication shops and ordered necessary equipment parts.

| Sept - May
1989 - 1990
1990 - 1991 | **UNIVERSITY OF ILLINOIS MACHINE SHOP**, Urbana, IL
Mechanical Engineer Research Machine Shop |

Shop Assistant

- Learned basic machining practices; performed basic maintenance on machine shop equipment.

- Operated: lathes, drill presses, bandsaw, bench presses, milling machines, sand blasters, surface grinders, cut-off saws.

- Worked in tool crib and assisted tool crib manager with record keeping.

ACTIVITIES

Project leader of the SAE Mini-Jeep

- Responsible for 20 students in the designing and fabrication of an all-terrain vehicle for competition against other universities.

Engineering Exposition, University of Illinois, 1988, 1990.

Speak and read fluent German.

KURT MULLENS
2310 Katy Court
Belle Chasse, LA 70037
(504) 555-8610

CAREER SUMMARY

Five years experience in foodservice distribution. Demonstrated expertise in devising marketing strategies, negotiating purchasing programs and managing inventory efficiently. Extensive knowledge in implementing marketing/purchasing objectives to achieve company goals. Strong leadership, interpersonal and motivational skills with team player attitude.

PROFESSIONAL EXPERIENCE

DYNAFOOD CORPORATION, Metairie, LA   Since 1987

<u>Product Manager</u>   Since 1991
Dynafood Corporate Headquarters, Metairie, LA

Managed, developed and negotiated national purchasing programs. Generated product promotions and implemented marketing objectives to foster sales and increase purchasing allowances. Informed and educated forty-five regional districts through initiating written directives and sales presentations.

- Collaboratively obtained a $5 million net gain in negotiated national purchasing programs.

- Designed labels, box shippers and point of sale material for private label program effectively increasing brand awareness.

- Devised strategies for product specifications tailored to national market preferences to generate a $7 million sales growth.

- Selected to conduct a special project which included orienting and training new purchasing personnel on a new computer system.

- Obtained certificate of training excellence by participating in "Powerful Presentation" seminar. Attended Lotus 1-2-3 two day workshops.

<u>Product Manager</u>   1990-1991
Dynafood Regional Service Center, St. Louis, MO

Managed inventory for regional locations. Controlled costs to meet regional profit objectives. Implemented national brand programs conducive to regional goals. Made presentations at procurement manager meetings to coordinate purchasing programs.

- Achieved and maintained a 99% order fill ratio, resulting in obtaining regional service level goal of 98.5%.

- Facilitated a new national brand program in three regional districts resulting in a $20,000 purchasing allowance during a three month period.

- Successfully gained expertise on commodity markets needed to achieve gross profit margins of 15%.

<u>Buyer/Merchandiser</u>   1987-1990
Dynafood Atlanta, Atlanta, GA

Marketed and purchased finished products; maintained price list and developed promotions/programs to reinforce marketing goals. Participated in sales meetings to educate, inform and motivate.

- Increased local promotional rebates by 15% through successful product promotions and new programs.

- Launched a new product category; accomplished a sales growth of 30% ($2 million) during the first six months.

- Superseded district goal of 28 day inventory level while accomplishing 99% order fill ratio.

- Member of the "District of the Year" awarded in 1987 for Metro South.

EDUCATION

B.B.A., Marketing, 1987
Tulane University
New Orleans, LA

F. CARL DONAHEY
216 Chad Road
Carlton, Washington 98814
Residence: (206) 555-2826
Office: (206) 555-6116

SUMMARY

Self-motivated professional with ten years of customer service experience. Imaginative problem solver with exceptional organizational skills. Team leader, motivator, and active participant. Proficient in IBM personal computer applications.

PROFESSIONAL EXPERIENCE

1987-1991   GENERAL AUTO ACCEPTANCE CORPORATION, Seattle, Washington

     1989-1991   *Senior Customer Account Representative*

        Supervised collection and customer service departments (nine employees). Resolved serious collection and customer service problems. Prepared reports for management.

- Developed relationships with key individuals within tribunal system. Resulted in first successful prosecution and repossession of vehicles while significantly reducing company write-offs of bad debts.

- Converted manual system to computer data base, which decreased follow-up time 25% and increased record keeping accuracy. Gained ability to generate reports for management in a fraction of the time previously spent.

- Initiated use of skip tracing firms. Attained 85% overall success rate in locating "hard core skips."

- Delegated responsibilities and cross-trained clerical staff on preliminary documentation of "skips" allowing collectors more productive time on phone.

     1987-1989   *Customer Accounts Representative*

        Collected and skip traced on 120 day plus retail accounts using an on-line terminal. Performed field collections, repossessions and dealer audits. Followed up on accounts assigned for repossession.

- Educated collection department personnel on statutes governing outside vendors. Allowed for better analysis of billings and ability to challenge erroneous charges while saving time and money.

- Trained staff in proper format for all correspondence. Introduced word processing capabilities which saved time and produced more professional documents.

- Successfully solicited subcontractor to collect from high risk, uncooperative consumers.

- Created repossession set-up document which reduced errors and saved review time.

1984-1987   **HANOVER SAVINGS AND LOAN, Brewster, Washington**

Financial Service Representative

Interviewed consumer loan applicants, performed credit analysis, and made recommendations for credit granting decisions. Opened and serviced savings accounts.

- Overcame competitors' marketing strategy by implementing unique campaign. Instituted personal approach tactics; resulted in capturing new business and providing community good will.

- Implemented weekly training to expand product awareness; established tracking system which motivated employees and increased referrals by 13 per quarter (50%).

- Established review of records; substantially impacted accuracy and reduced customer conflicts and litigation.

- Conducted promotion, soliciting merchant donations; increased visibility and patronage which expanded ATM usage by 20%.

- Eliminated chaos in file storage area by reorganizing files and disposing of lapsed records. Increased access ability and information utilization previously unattainable.

EDUCATION

B.S., Pepperdine College, Los Angeles, CA, 1986
Finance, Computer Science Emphasis

ELLEN GAMBLE
1520 Army Trail, Apartment 36F
Crystal City, MO 63019
(314) 555-3606

SUMMARY

Eighteen years experience in administrative office environment utilizing wide variety of general office and computer skills. Ability to successfully interact with people at all levels in academic and business environments.

PROFESSIONAL EXPERIENCE

CAM DATA CORPORATION   **1989 - 1992**
Clayton, MO

Administrative Assistant
Initially started as temporary and transitioned to full time employee status. Administrative support position in office of 32 employees. Accountable for travel reservations, workshops, seminars, purchase requisitions, invoices, all general office machines, office supplies and vendors.

- Helped design system to track off-site purchase orders 90% faster.

- Coordinated use of recycled materials purchased reducing costs $3500 in one category.

- Assisted in authorship of first off-site procedures manual for St. Louis operating office.

- Designed travel report combining multi-source information into one report.

WASHINGTON UNIVERSITY   **1978 - 1989**
St. Louis, MO

Senior Administrative Secretary   1985 - 1989
Administrative Secretary   1978 - 1985
Directly responsible for office management of two aeronautical engineering professors and nine students plus flexibility to assume additional tasks from twelve other department professors and their students. Handled preparation of theses, documents, grant proposals, contract reports and technical papers. Responsible for seminar speakers and all travel arrangements. Successfully interacted with visitors, faculty, students and staff from diverse backgrounds.

- Oversaw budgets, contracts, professional contacts, correspondence and scheduling while supervisor was on six-month sabbatical out of the country.

- Implemented tracking of prospective journal articles and all communications with authors.

- Assisted editor and publisher in preparation and publication of invited lectures for international symposium.

- Coordinated weekly technical film series with professors and class schedules.

FIRST BANK OF MISSOURI   **1975 - 1978**
St. Louis, MO

Personal Secretary for Office Manager/Office Personnel Secretary
General secretarial position for bank department handling delinquent personal property loans. Handled all personnel records for 15 member office and batch processing of incoming payments, daily ledger balancing and overflow from documents to desk. Coordinated and scheduled inventory by bank personnel of automobile dealer stock on hand.

NCA FINANCE CORPORATION   **1971 - 1972**
Cranford, NJ and New Haven, CT

Head Cashier
Head cashier in small loan office responsible for all loan paperwork including clearing credit reports. In charge of all cash in office, daily balancing of payments, reports to main office and customer interaction. Supervised staff. In absence of office manager, in charge of all office decisions including loan approvals.

EDUCATION

B.A., Psychology, Illinois State University, Bloomington, IL 1975

COMPUTER SKILLS

Microsoft Word for Mac	Excel
Power Point	WordPerfect
MacDraw	Lotus 1-2-3

JACOB P. HODGES

16 Mary Frances Place
Raleigh, NC 27606

Residence: (919) 555-9006
Office: (919) 555-0968

SUMMARY OF QUALIFICATIONS

Strong computer and operations management skills developed during twelve years of post-college work experience with both mainframe systems and personal computers in a manufacturing environment. Able to understand business problems, apply automated solutions, and provide training. Candidate for M.B.A. in Management Information Systems.

EXPERIENCE AND ACCOMPLISHMENTS

HWB, INC., Research Triangle Park, NC   1981 - Present
Space Avionics Division

Senior Inventory Planner   1986 - Present

- Managed inventory levels and availability of complex, cost-intensive, Commercial Test Equipment worth over $14 million to meet production requirements for avionics test systems. Controlled production activities through use of in-house computer systems, including IBM PC/XT/AT, Macintosh and an MRP-II system on the mainframe.

- Trained employees on the MRP system when it was installed and assisted in the "Beta testing" of a procurement sub-system when it was added. Co-authored many of the user manuals for the new system. Served on a council which prioritized system change requests for the Information Systems department.

- Programmed in dBase-III for several PC-based applications on IBM PC/XT/AT. Used query languages to create special reports using data from the mainframe systems.

Military and Strategic Avionics Division, Dayton, OH

Senior Systems Coordinator   1981-1986

- Managed production control tasks with automated production and inventory control systems applied to the manufacture of avionics test equipment. Performed cost/schedule reporting.

- Trained new employees. Reported to customers in monthly reviews. Developed new applications for personal computers.

DYNAMIC SYSTEMS, INC., Raleigh, NC   1979 - 1981
Data Systems Division

Sales Administrator

- Coordinated customer sales orders for specialized test equipment; supported staff of nine sales representatives.

- Interacted with engineering department to determine customer requirements.

- Performed sales forecasts which were used to set production levels.

EDUCATION

B.A., **Duke University**, Durham, North Carolina, 1978
College of Liberal Arts and Institute of Technology

- Strong math and science background

M.B.A. candidate, **Duke University**, Durham, North Carolina
Management Information Systems

- Operations Management
- Structured Analysis and Design
- Data Modeling
- End User Computing
- Decision Support Systems
- Telecommunications

Advanced Coursework

Basic, Pascal, C, Assembly Language, and fourth generation query languages

BYRON GARDNER
609 Jackson Street
Pasadena, CA 91101
(818) 555-1848

QUALIFICATIONS SUMMARY

Over thirteen years management and supervisory experience in manufacturing and distribution with a consistent record of increasing productivity and problem solving. Extensive experience in all facets of warehouse operations. Further experience in safety management, policy administration, security procedures, personnel development, planning, scheduling and manufacturing.

PROFESSIONAL EXPERIENCE

1977-1991   **ABRITE BATTERY COMPANY, INC.,** Columbus, Ohio

    1988-1991   <u>Assistant Warehouse Manager</u>, La Cresenta, CA

        Responsible for day to day operations and security of an 120,000 square foot warehouse containing $200M inventory.

- Supervised 18 warehouse and 6 office employees. Trained all new employees in company and warehouse operating procedures. Maintained the highest overall efficiency of all company warehouses.

- Coordinated all inbound and outbound freight. Set up and maintained inventory schedules.

- Revised warehouse stock location system that reduced operator cost and improved shipping time goals.

- Restructured warehouse through realignment of duties and personnel eliminating 6,000 manpower hours annually.

- Directed warehouse safety program. Set up interactive one-on-one employee sessions to increase employee involvement and reduce operation problems.

    1983-1988   <u>Department Supervisor</u>, Columbus Ohio

        Responsible for two electrode manufacturing departments, one paper and metal processing department.

- Supervised 40 people across three shifts in three departments. Set up monthly production schedules and led action team meetings between engineering groups and production.

- Maintained all plant and OSHA Safety Regulations in hazardous environment and retained required records. Updated all safety equipment in department.

- Improved Department efficiency by 15%, while reducing manpower 4% and scrap by 5%.

1979-1983   Foreman, Columbus, Ohio

Responsible for Nickel Cadmium and Carbon Raw Cell assembly and finishing department.

- Supervised 25-36 employees across two shifts and seven different departments in assembly line operations.

- Conducted weekly departmental safety meetings. Administered attendance, safety, payroll and production policy and procedures.

- Maintained inventory of raw materials for assembly and all support operations across three shifts.

1977-1979   Material Handler, La Cresenta, CA

Extensive background in material handling shipping, receiving and warehousing. Also, experience in fork lift truck operations, maintaining inventory and U.P.S. machine. Experience as a shipping, bill of lading and receiving clerk.

EDUCATION

B.A., Ambassador College, Pasadena, CA, Psychology/Social Science, 1976

MARY ANN McCLOSKEY

26 Barnett Road
Toronto, Ontario
M8W 5J8

Res: (416) 555-7891

Retail marketing manager with extensive experience for one of Canada's largest retailers in promotions, customer service, in-store merchandising and sales. Intuitively creative visual presentation technique combined with strong planning and organizational skills. Strong fashion flair with a talent for pulling a look together.

PROFESSIONAL EXPERIENCE

BIG STORE INC., Etobicoke, Ontario   **1986-1991**
Sales Manager

Marketing

▸ Managed 40,000 sq.ft. fashion floor with annual sales in excess of $10 million.

▸ Developed visual presentation for total "look" of fashion floor which shifted focus from exploitation to Lifestyle merchandising, yielding increased gross profit.

▸ Executed ads which exploited regular priced merchandise in Lifestyle concept consistent with new marketing strategy.

Promotions

▸ Successfully organized fashion show production for audience of 500. Worked directly with models, media, advertising. Improved company's overall fashion profile.

▸ Coordinated in-store accessory fair in cosmetic, jewelery, shoes and acccessory divisions with vendor participation. Won first prize for overall project out of 20 stores.

Customer Service

▸ Coached team of 15 management personnel and over 200 sales associates to achieve 100% in customer service as measured through surveys of professional shoppers.

▸ Resolved a broad range of customer problems by dealing sensitively and quickly on a one-on-one basis with individuals, enhancing public relations for the company.

SUPER MALL, Calgary, British Columbia   **1985**
Manager

Marketing

▸ Instrumental in all aspects of successful set up and establishment of five independent high profile boutiques within extremely tight time constraints.

▸ Implemented training for staff of 40 in regard to in-store marketing, window displays and product knowledge.

Administration

▸ Communicated as liaison for out-of-city owners with mall administration, media and brokers regarding all business transactions.

▸ Hired, coached and managed staff of 40.

LADIESWEAR CANADA, Toronto, Ontario   **1982-1985**
Manager

Marketing

▸ Developed "fashion" profile in moderate price zone using visual presentation skills and in-store marketing, resulting in significantly increased sales for moderately priced merchandise.

▸ Participated on Super Mall advisory board and contributed directly to the total mall image.

▸ Decreased expense costs and increased overall annual sales by 10% through coaching and team building of direct staff of 12.

EDUCATION

Fashion and Merchandising Diploma, **Ryerson Polytechnical Institute**, Toronto, Ontario, 1982

Professional Seminars:

Time Management/Coaching   In-Store Marketing
Communication/Retail Marketing   Personnel Training
Profiling/Basics Inventory   Stock Shortage

ALYCE M. CHU

771 South Linden Avenue
Stamford, CT 06907
(203) 555-4314

**CAREER
SUMMARY**

Communication professional skilled at designing and directing results-oriented, cost-effective programs for sales promotion, advertising, public relations, corporate meeting planning and speaker support. Proven ability to position companies as industry leaders through internal and external marketing efforts.

**PROFESSIONAL
EXPERIENCE**

INFO DATA, INC., Stamford, CT   1986 to Present
A General & Forrester Corporation company

Manager, Advertising and Collateral   1989 to Present
Managed advertising campaign, corporate graphic standards, and collateral program.

- Developed annual corporate advertising strategy and directed ad agency in all facets of implementation.

- Designed and implemented project and budget tracking system which brought collateral program in on time and on budget.

- Instituted corporate graphic standards to ensure a cohesive collateral and image campaign.

Manager, Internal Communications   1986 to 1989
Organized, staffed and managed start-up department to provide cost-effective internal marketing and communication vehicles.

- Reduced production costs by 50% on a per project basis, totaling $15,000 for first year.

- Recommended and implemented the purchase of Macintosh equipment in an entirely IBM environment; devised cost-effective delivery vehicles through two-tier process.

- Externally recognized as expert in desktop publishing field; appeared in premier issues of Macintosh Business Review and was invited to speak on the subject "Macintosh in Marketing."

LUNDE SWEETS, INC., Belmont, MA   1978 to 1986

Sales Promotion Assistant

- Increased and sustained customer base and consumer loyalty through coupon programs and sweepstakes.

- Bought placements in magazines and newspapers for all product lines; increased overall product recognition while staying under budget.

- Assessed artwork and copy from ad agencies and promotion houses for appropriateness and accuracy.

EDUCATION

Mount Saint James High School, Worcester, MA
Diploma, 1970

Additional Coursework

Essentials of Management
Dynamic Graphics - Advanced Electronic Design
Consolidated Papers Seminar
Corporate Electronics Publishing Systems Seminars
Creative Conferences
Apple Forum
Desktop Publishing Symposium

COMMUNITY INVOLVEMENT

Provided pro bono artwork for the American Cancer Society "Taste of Tomorrow" benefit

Designed flyer for the Belmont "Frontier Days Festival"

Solicitor for the United Way Campaign

63½ BEVERLY LANE
DALLAS, TX 75205
(214) 555-1360

BACKGROUND SUMMARY

Attorney with extensive corporate law, corporate secretarial and private law firm experience. Related areas of involvement include:

- Public & Private Offerings
- Financings
- Acquisitions and Divestitures
- S.E.C. Compliance
- Commercial Contracts
- General Corporate

EDUCATION

J.D., YALE UNIVERSITY, New Haven, CT, 1975
Participant: Moot Court Competition
Concentration: Corporation and Securities Law

B.A., CORNELL UNIVERSITY, Ithaca, NY, 1972
Honors degree in Politics

CAREER HISTORY

BCE PRODUCTS CORPORATION, Dallas, TX   Since 1983
A diversified Fortune 300 company, whose businesses included agricultural products and services, mining, construction materials and equipment leasing.

<u>**Vice President, Corporate Secretary and Associate General Counsel**</u>

Financings, Acquisitions and Divestitures

Directed general corporate legal matters, including review, negotiation, documentation and advice to senior management on public and private offerings of equity and debt, loan and other credit agreements, acquisitions and divestitures, joint ventures.

Securities

Managed all phases of U.S. and Canadian securities law compliance, including preparation and legal review of Securities Act registration statements, Securities Exchange Act annual and periodic reports, proxy statements, stock exchange listings and maintenance; advised on public disclosure issues and public relations matters.

Employee Plans and Policies

Reviewed and advised on human resources issues, policies and codes of conduct, benefit plans and agreements, including stock option, deferred compensation, employment agreements, severance agreements, consulting agreements; and internal legal review of pension plans. Wrote computer program for administration of stock benefit plans.

General Corporate

Negotiated and prepared contracts for commercial transactions, stockholders agreements, real estate subleases; reviewed and advised on insurance matters, including coordinating preparation of applications for general liability and directors and officers liability coverage, and claims issues.

Legal Administration

Handled or supervised all aspects of corporate secretarial function, including:

- *Board of Directors*: Provided preparation and legal review of content of agenda and materials for board of directors' and committee meetings, and preparation and legal review of minutes; proper authorization of all corporate actions.

- *Stockholders*: Coordinated all matters relating to meetings, including preparation of annual affiliates' information questionnaire, proxy statement, response to stockholder proposals, SEC clearance; managed proxy solicitation and tabulation process; obtained and maintained stock exchange listings.

- *General*: Supervised corporate housekeeping function, including incorporation, qualification and maintenance of subsidiaries and affiliates, and departmental records retention.

CASEY, ADAMS AND CORLESS, New York, NY 1975 to 1983
A 265-lawyer firm with a diverse corporate and litigation practice.

<u>Associate</u>

Engaged in general corporate practice, with emphasis on securities law and mergers and acquisitions, including: public offerings of equity and debt securities, tender offers and exchange offers, restructuring and recapitalization; merger, stock purchase and asset purchase agreements, "due diligence" investigations; confidentiality agreements; partnership agreements; stockholder buy-outs and repurchases.

PROFESSIONAL

BAR ADMISSION: 1976, California, New York, Texas
MEMBER: American Bar Association, Association of the Bar of the City of Dallas, National Bar Association, American Society of Corporate Secretaries.

ANDREA ANSON TAYLOR
21 Oakdale Lane
Belle Meade, TN 37205

Residence: (615) 555-6116
Office: (615) 555-8100

EXECUTIVE SUMMARY

A senior human resources executive with extensive corporate and consulting experience in organizational development, analysis, design, developing performance management systems and a broad range of human resource management program implementation and operation.

PROFESSIONAL EXPERIENCE

VICE PRESIDENT HUMAN RESOURCES & ADMINISTRATION   1989 - 1992
Spectrum Music, Inc., Nashville, Tennessee

Headed corporate wide human resources programs for this $700 million/2,500 employee recording company.   Reported to CEO and managed professional staff of over 100 in organizational development, compensation and benefits management, recruiting, training and a variety of other human resources functions. Directed all facilities and space management groups, corporate graphics, travel services function and served on the corporate business acquisitions committee.   Also functioned as senior operating and administrative executive for studio operations. Produced over $5.2 million in revenues and $1.2 million in profits.   Selected achievements during this period include:

- Directed acquisition of jazz music label into the corporation, increasing sales from $12 million to $45 million and profits from breakeven to $4.2 million.

- Restructured travel service programs resulting in $600,000 annual savings.

- Reorganized studio department operations resulting in a $300,000 increase in sales and a $200,000 increase in profits.

- Developed special staff support program that resulted in an annual reduction of $257,000 for temporary personnel.

PRESIDENT   1985 - 1989
Human Resources Dynamics, Inc., Minneapolis, MN

Served a variety of clients in providing a broad range of human resource consulting services. Acted operationally as Vice President Human Resources for $70 million restaurant chain, Blue Range Restaurants. Implemented several programs including:

- Developed and implemented the strategic planning process.

- Installed a flexible benefits program and an HRIS system.

- Restructured Field Operations and redefined accountabilities and performance measures for Operations.

VICE PRESIDENT HUMAN RESOURCES 1983 - 1985
Pizza World, Inc., Minneapolis, MN

Chief Human Resources Officer reporting to the President and CEO of this $300 million 860 unit restaurant chain. Directed a professional staff in all of the responsibilities of a large human resources group including, organizational development, compensation and benefits, corporate and field training, job evaluation and incentive program development. Installed a total compensation program which included job evaluation and incentive programs. Implemented a major field operations training program for the units.

TAFT, INC. 1976 - 1983

VICE PRESIDENT PERSONNEL, 1981 - 1983
Western America Van Lines Inc., Madison, Wisconsin

Reported to the President and directed the employee relations function of this $500 million division of Taft, Inc. Promoted to this position to bring about organizational change following the deregulation of the trucking industry.

SENIOR DIRECTOR FIELD PERSONNEL, 1978 - 1981
Pizza Bites, Inc. Norfolk, VA

Directed the activities of four Division Personnel Managers and 13 Regional Managers for this $500 million division with 4,000 stores and 22,000 employees. Rose to this position from a role as Senior Director of Management Development.

ASSOCIATE MANAGER, MANAGER DEVELOPMENT, May 1976 - April 1978
Goody, Inc., *formerly known as Goodman Western Foods, Inc.*, Costa, Mesa, CA

Provided on-site consultation to over 30 plants and 15 sales divisions as a corporate psychologist for this $2 billion consumer foods manufacturer.

DIRECTOR OF TRAINING 1974 - 1976
Westwood Medical Center, Westwood, CA

Directed the hospital wide training programs of this 750 bed teaching hospital with 1,900 employees.

EDUCATION

PhD, Counseling Psychology, University of California at Los Angeles, 1974
MA, Educational Psychology & Measurements, University of California at Los Angeles, 1971
BA, Psychology & Sociology, Stanford University, Stanford, California, 1968

OTHER INTERESTS

Instructor for Vanderbilt University, Nashville, Tennessee. Subjects include: Personnel Management, Industrial Psychology and Organizational Behavior.

MICHAEL W. SHEFCYK

2242 Ewing Circle North
Edina, MN 55424

Residence: (612) 555-2401
Office: (612) 555-4876

Manufacturing Division Manager with a record of innovation and accomplishment in the thin film coating industry. Experienced in product development, manufacturing, operations, production control, quality assurance, engineering, marketing and sales and P&L accountability for organizing and developing new business units into profitable entities.

PROFESSIONAL EXPERIENCE

AOC LABORATORIES, St. Louis Park, MN   **1972-1991**

Ophthalmic Program Director   **1988-1991**

- Prepared and implemented business plan for manufacture of high performance sunglasses. Developed and implemented business strategy for company's entry into Ophthalmic market. Created national sales organization.

- Successfully renegotiated multi-million dollar contract with major customer who failed to meet contractual commitments affecting company's ability to produce and deliver product on timely basis.

Business Unit Manager   **1984-1987**

- Directed company's first entry into after market business. P&L responsibility for business unit employing 65 staff and production members. Managed operating budget of $3 million and marketing effort producing $9 million in annual sales.

- Established partnership with another company to develop new distribution strategy. Successfully entered 5 new marketing channels. Currently market leader in 4 channels.

- Directed team of engineers and marketing specialists to find alternatives to costly manufacturing process subject to rapid change in technology. Developed vacuum form method enabling new product introduction. Now market leader.

- Reorganized work flow to maximize use of limited floor space and instituted on-time deliveries by suppliers to reduce materials inventories and working capital requirements.

Manufacturing Manager   **1981-1984**

- Managed most profitable department in company. P&L responsibility to gross margin level for manufacture of laminated filters product line. Directed staff of 35. Annual sales of $8 million.

- Assembled team of engineers, production workers, quality assurance and sales people from company and elicited customer participation to analyze costly reject problem. Increased company yields from 64% to 92%.

Department Manager   **1976-1981**

- Supervised 12 staff and production members operating three coating machines producing thin film coats on customer furnished materials. Maintained product quality, schedules, cost effective operation, safety, and high level of staff proficiency.

Lead Coating Machine Operator   **1972-1976**

- Supervised two other coating machine operators on swing shift. Attended University of Minnesota.

AFFILIATIONS

Member Board of Directors, Forest Lake Industries, Eden Prairie, MN

EDUCATION

M.B.A., Finance, Marketing, Organization Development, 1989.
University of Minnesota, Minneapolis, MN

B.A., Marketing, 1981.
University of Minnesota, Minneapolis, MN

Certificates of Completion

Statistical Process Control and Quality Improvement
Just-in-Time Techniques
Total Quality Control
World Class Manufacturing

SKILLS

PC literate: Word processing and spreadsheets

LANCE F. ROBINSON
62 Nancy Court
Highland Park, IL 60035
Residence: (708) 555-3612
Office: (312) 555-0125

QUALIFICATIONS SUMMARY

Executive with rapid and consistent record of growth and advancement for domestic and international airlines. Adept at directing large and small organizations, consistently exceeding performance and profit projections. Excellent long and short-range planning skills.

PROFILE SUMMARY

- Seasoned sales, marketing and operations senior manager
- Skilled at developing and overseeing complex assignments involving planning, financial controls and sales
- Proven team builder and leader in senior staff and line management positions
- Successful record of turning around problem operations and start-ups.
- Highly developed presentation and writing skills

PROFESSIONAL EXPERIENCE

1988 - Present   WORLD AIRLINES, Chicago, IL

   1990 - Present   <u>Vice President, National Sales, The Americas</u>

Headed start up of new national sales organization for the Americas with staff of over 24 and $125 million in revenues.

- Formulated marketing plans, strategies and budgets within 60 days. Accountable for revenues of $215 million under an operating budget of $2.3 million.

- As member of Senior Management Planning Committee, participated in all strategy and planning decisions. Prepared short and long term tactical strategies involving response to competitive threats and marketing opportunities.

   1989-1990   <u>Vice President, Reservations, The Americas</u>

Assigned to turn around World Airlines' North American reservations centers located in Chicago and Toronto. Completely reorganized organization by reducing of one level of supervision, reinstating accountability and smaller supervisor to agent ratios.

- Successfully reversed declines in productivity, attendance and discipline. Increased sales by $1.2 million in 8 months.

- Won 1990 "Best Sales Support Organization in The Americas" award for renewed ability to provide best service to our public, industry and internal customers.

1988-1989   <u>Regional Manager Passenger Sales, Northwest USA</u>

Directed staff of twelve, including district sales managers, account executives, supervisory and sales administration personnel.

- Generated sales of $25 million; increased revenues by $7 million in 1987.

- Introduced Account Partnering concept to local sales force, which was adopted by the Americas region as preferred selling strategy.

- Chaired the Override Commission Task Force, which restructured override schedules and reviewed ways to expedite payment to key wholesale customers. Reduced annual costs by $5 million.

1965-1988   ATLANTIC AIR, INC., San Francisco, CA & New York, NY

1976-1988   <u>Manager Passenger Sales</u>

Led Direct Sales and Marketing for the seventh largest revenue generating city in the Atlantic Air system. Annual revenues of $149 million and staff of 38 management and non-management personnel.

- Created Association Sales program which generated over $10.8 million in annual incremental revenue. Duplicated in all sales regions within Atlantic Air.

- In 1988, won the appointment of Atlantic Air as official carrier for both Republican and Democratic National Conventions—a first in the airline industry and valued at $9.6 million.

- Received the Distinguished Sales Award from Sales and Marketing Executives of Washington, D.C. in 1984. Featured in July, 1985 issue of *Association Management* magazine, as member of ASAE's Executive Roundtable.

1974-1976   <u>Manager Forecasts & Quotas</u>

1972-1974   <u>Industrial Engineer, Finance & Budgets</u>

1969-1972   <u>Area Sales Manager, Passenger Sales</u>

1965-1969   <u>Staff Analyst, Corporate Marketing</u>

EDUCATION

1990, M.B.A., Roosevelt University, Chicago, IL, Academic Emphasis on Finance & Marketing.

1965, B.A., Pomona College, Pomona, CA, Majors in History & PreMedicine.

KARA E. JAMES

36 Crystal Court
Denver, CO 80206

Home: (303) 555-2662
Messages: (303) 555-4000

SUMMARY OF QUALIFICATIONS

Successful hospital executive in not-for-profit health care institutions. Proven results in high stress and "turnaround" situations, primarily in community, teaching/research and public institutions of approximately 400 beds with wide range of services, including extensive out-patient programs.

EXPERIENCE/SELECTED PROFESSIONAL ACCOMPLISHMENTS

MT. SINAI GENERAL HOSPITAL, Denver, CO.   **1984 - present**
A 380 bed, community, hospital with annual revenue of $70MM and 1200 employees.

Chief Operating Officer. Directed budget, staffing and programs for all hospital departments through three Vice Presidents, as well as the specific departments of Radiology, Pathology, Cardiology, Risk Management/Quality Assurance, Personnel, Building Services and Management Information Service. Provided staffing for all medical staff committees.

- Headed day-to-day operation of hospital, generating an average excess of revenue over expenses of 3.20% over six years with a range of 0.7% in 1985 to 7.2% in 1990. Last five years excess revenue over expenses averaged 4.2%.

- Directed $30MM new construction and renovation project, including a new 20-bed intensive care unit, expanded rehabilitation facility, ambulatory surgery center, cardiac catheterization, laboratory, MRI suite and major renovation/expansion of emergency room.

- Developed strategic plan and program for opening Emergency Services Department, projected increase of 7,000 emergency room visits and 400 admissions annually with an additional $4MM revenue by 1992.

ST. LUKES MEDICAL CENTER, San Francisco, CA   **1975 - 1984**
A 460-bed, city/county owned, teaching hospital for University of California with annual revenues of $40MM and 1500 employees; union environment.

Acting Executive Director/Assistant Executive Director. Directed budget, staffing and programs for thirteen departments with a budget of approximately $25 million.

- Key participant in developing strategy; served on negotiating committee for three sets of labor contract negotiations with the hospital worker's union. Developed and implemented strike plan, enabling the hospital to operate through 19-day work stoppage.

- Developed regional Perinatal Center that provided 90% of the region's perinatal health services (100 mile radius). Doubled deliveries to 4,000 annually.

EDUCATION

M.S. Health Care Administration, Boston University, Boston, MA, 1968
B.A., Sociology, Coe College, Cedar Rapids, Iowa, 1967

Combination Resumes

JUDITH M. OXFORD
832 Brookhollow Drive
Tyler, TX 75707
(903) 555-0356

SUMMARY OF QUALIFICATIONS

Five years of diversified business experience in both the service and manufacturing industries, encompassing areas in Sales, Marketing, Purchasing, Customer Service, Credit and Collections. Proficient in a systems environment, including CRT and word processing. Extremely organized, detail-oriented with excellent communication and negotiation skills.

SELECTED ACCOMPLISHMENTS

Sales

- ▸ Maintained small accounts in Southwest region, grossing approximately $550,000 annually in sales.

- ▸ Developed leads for outside sales reps using telemarketing techniques. Team effort increased new business in region by over 30 percent.

- ▸ Implemented promotion of new product to current accounts through mail and telephone campaign. As a result, product's first quarter revenues exceeded predictions by $53,000.

- ▸ Won divisional "Deal of the Month" contest two times.

Purchasing

- ▸ Negotiated volume discounts that resulted in savings of over $25,000 per year.

- ▸ Started preferred vendor relationships with three new vendors, resulting in higher quality service and projected savings of $150,000 over a three year period.

- ▸ Consistently met departmental goals by maintaining prompt turnaround and staying within budget.

Customer Relations

- ▸ Resolved billing dispute with major client that resulted in full collection of past due receivables ($15.5K) while maintaining a profitable relationship with the client.

- ▸ Implemented a follow-up service questionnaire to evaluate customer satisfaction with the help they received. An average of 90% of the customers indicated that they were satisfied or very satisfied.

- ▸ Prepared comprehensive customer service manual and trained new department reps.

Administration

- ▸ Received, processed and entered orders into computer. Achieved same day turnaround on 99% of the orders.

- ▸ Developed a centralized and accurate product/vendor library which helped reduce the average purchasing cycle time by two days.

- ▸ Updated and corrected health club membership accounts on computer. Kept updates current during growth period when membership doubled.

PROFESSIONAL HISTORY

1991- Present	**CROWN QUIGLEY**, Tyler, TX Purchasing Agent
1989- 1991	**FRANCK CORPORATION**, Irving, TX Sales Assistant
1986- 1988	**TANDEM HEALTH & FITNESS CORPORATION**, Highland Park, TX Customer Service

EDUCATION

B.S., **Baylor University**, Waco, TX, 1986
Biology & Anthropology Double Major

Customer Complaint Certification, **Dun & Bradstreet**

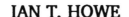

9000 Blossom Blvd.
Lawton, Oklahoma 73501

Residence (909) 555-6321
Office (909) 555-9234

SUMMARY OF EXPERIENCE

Plant/Operations Manager with strong manufacturing experience at facilities of 1,200+ employees with increasing managerial responsibilities in technical support operations, engineering, tool room, and maintenance production. Achieved most significant results in: start up, expansion and new system installation; facilities planning; developing an integral role for the technical staff in the manufacturing operations; and developing subordinates.

Functional skills critical to major successes:
- Thorough project analysis and evaluation
- Team building, motivating and developing others
- Setting and attaining specific and measurable objectives
- Diplomacy and patience to successfully implement long term plans

SELECTED ACCOMPLISHMENTS

Implementation of Long-term Project
Initiated major changes in manufacturing to fully utilize J.I.T. principles at largest of company's four U.S. plants. Automated 40% of molding presses, consolidated 30% of fabrication operations onto assembly lines or into molding, and directly linked 25% of assembly lines to molding presses. Received company Special Achievement Award (1987). Awarded national recognition by Association for Manufacturing Excellence and spotlighted on Fall 1989 Executive Tour.

Computerized Budget Process
Introduced plant-wide computerized budgeting replacing manual data entry. Developed computerized budgets in tool room, production, and maintenance departments. Generated annual operating plans, linking up directly to controller's master plant budget. Reduced four day roll up process into few hours, improving accuracy and responsiveness.

Defeat of Union
Stopped repeated attempts in 1989-91 to unionize the Lawton, Oklahoma plant. Strengthened non-union position; enhanced first line supervisors' awareness of legal limits and obligations, and increased level of employee/management communication. Achieved support of non-union status by majority of workers.

Facilities Expansion
Directed major production and molding expansion at Iowa City plant. Increased production output by 40%; increased molding shop to 78 machines.

EMPLOYMENT EXPERIENCE

KID'S STUFF, Oklahoma City, OK **1970-1991**
One of the top four manufacturers of children's toys and juvenile/infant products; recognized as one of the top three in 1989 survey of 91 major brand products for value/quality. A $700 million division of Playtime Company.

PLANT SUPERINTENDENT, Lawton, OK **1988-1991**
Managed up to nine direct reports and 1,200 employees in plastics molding, fabrication, assembly, engineering, tool room and maintenance; 78 molding machines and 20 assembly lines; operating budgets in excess of $20 million annually.

TECHNICAL SERVICES MANAGER, Lawton, OK **1985-1988**
Managed engineering, tool room and maintenance departments at this 1,500 employee plant. Directed 95 people in various work groups/levels; 40 molding machines and 25 assembly lines; operating budgets exceeding $5 million/year; capital plan of $.05 million/year.

ENGINEERING MANAGER, Iowa City, IA **1980-1984**
Supervised fourteen manufacturing, industrial and plastics engineering personnel. Provided support to all plant operations including new product start ups. Operating budget of $600K/year. Saved $1.2 million annually.

SUPERVISOR OF ENGINEERING, Iowa City, IA **1972-1980**
Directed eight employees in manufacturing and industrial engineering departments. Provided technical support to fabrication, assembly and injection molding units.

MANUFACTURING ENGINEER, Iowa City, IA **1970-1972**
Provided engineering support for new plant start up, conducted training, and debugged tools and production equipment. Brought company's first vacuum form tooling and equipment into operation. Expanded staff from one to five. Rewrote parts specification book for over 1,000 molded items used for manufacturing.

EDUCATION

M.B.A., General Management, **University of Iowa,** Iowa City, 1973
B.M.E., Mechanical Design, **University of Iowa,** Iowa City, 1970
    2nd Lt., U.S. Army Ordnance Corps ROTC, 1970
    Co-op Student with Kid's Stuff, 1967-1970
    National and Mechanical Engineering Honor Fraternities

PROFESSIONAL AND COMMUNITY INVOLVEMENT

Industry Advisory Council, Iowa University
Vice President, Board of Directors, Lawton Public Library

DWIGHT COLEMAN

1334 Cruz Crossing Road
Anderson, MD 21285

Residence: (301) 555-3752
Office: (301) 555-4026

SUMMARY

Senior executive with over 18 years of management, sales, and marketing experience. Innovative team leader in developing strategies responsive to changing market trends. Successfully achieved business plan objectives with year after year production increases.

KEY ACCOMPLISHMENTS

MANAGEMENT

- Designed and implemented new "pay at risk" manager compensation plan.

- Reduced operating expenses by $900,000 through staff reductions, elimination of duplicate support units and reorganization of field management team.

- Instituted new fee that netted the company in excess of $2 million in first three years.

- Led transition to sales culture through the implementation of a proactive sales management training program. The number of marginal sales managers was reduced from nine to one.

STRATEGIC PLANNING

- As a member of the management team, developed business plan objectives and strategies for a $16 billion division with increases in profitability for past three years.

- Realigned organization structure so that the functions of training, technical support and marketing reported directly to sales management. Substantially reduced the response time to take advantage of market opportunities and to resolve customer service issues.

- Designed new support system that significantly increased customer contact time for the sales force.

SALES AND MARKETING

- Introduced "Executive in the field" day featuring the president in a program designed to align executive strategic planners with day-to-day market and operational conditions. Outcome provided processing, pricing and marketing changes resulting in a $1.6 million increase in sales.

- Increased production by 23% with the installation of a centralized processing system, introduction of a commission based sales force, and the development of a comprehensive sales training program.

- Implemented service philosophy to provide focus for service and sales culture. Recognized as only major company in Top Ten for customer service by independent consumer group.

- Selected and developed two area sales managers that in two years were rated number one and two out of eight in sales production.

EXPERIENCE

AMERICAN FEDERAL BANK, Baltimore, MD   1972-1991

Senior Vice President & Regional Manager   1987-1991

Supervised up to five area sales managers and 72 officers with a $28 million operating budget. Production responsibilities for residential lending, consumer lending and deposit acquisition.

Area Sales Manager   1978-1987

Supervised 20 offices with production responsibility for residential lending and deposit acquisition.

Bank Manager   1972-1978

Managed major second city unit; supervised all bank operations. Won "Manager Award" for best performance 1974 and 1975.

EDUCATION

B.S. Degree in Management, 1966
University of Tampa, Tampa FL

MILITARY

U.S. Air Force, 1967-1972
Separated with rank of Captain

AFFILIATIONS

Board of Directors, Chamber of Commerce
President, Rotary Club
Board of Directors, Greater Baltimore YMCA
Board of Directors, AmeriFed Insurance

Functional Resumes

PAMELA BEYER

1742 Ballard Street
Poway, CA
(714) 555-4197

CAREER SUMMARY

Over twelve years experience as a sales and marketing professional, holding increasingly responsible positions. Demonstrated outstanding organizational skills, combined with a high level of creative energy. At ease handling multiple projects at the same time with equal competency. Viewed by clients as a knowledgeable, reliable, and resourceful person with a very positive attitude.

PROFESSIONAL EXPERIENCE and ACCOMPLISHMENTS

Sales and Marketing

- Built a diversified client base of repeat and new business which resulted in consistent sales volume from $300,000 to $1 million in three year period.

- Systematized a highly effective quick response program for customers which resulted in repeat business and increased sales.

- Designed innovative marketing tools for sales staff which improved customer relationships.

- Handled all phases of project management for clients on local, national and international levels, resulting in a reputation for competent, reliable personalized service.

- Increased sales by working closely with architects and designers to meet specific customer product specifications.

- Made presentations to major architectural and design firms for the purpose of developing strong business relationships.

- Developed and implemented a marketing plan to increase sales leads, stimulate new sales and increase company's profits.

- Integrated new sales programs with Architect, Interior Design and Engineering firms.

- Served as company Public Relations Representative to professional organizations.

- Planned corporate events and trade shows attended by local professionals.

- Developed and implemented advertising campaigns.

<u>Management Skills</u>

- Trained and oriented 46 dealer representatives on furniture products.

- Designed, coordinated and conducted seminars on various subjects.

- Managed and developed a 650 square mile sales territory.

EDUCATION and PROFESSIONAL DEVELOPMENT

- B.A., Education, Eureka College, Eureka, California
- A.A., Interior Design, Pasadena City College, Pasadena, California
- Professional Selling Skills / Strategic Selling Skills / Psychology of Achievement

INTERESTS

Music, Docent for the Art Institute, Ice Skating

Sample Letters

Executive Recruiter

NICHOLAS P. ROSSINI

18640 Jaffe Drive
Colorado Springs, CO 80906
(719) 555-0024

Date

Mr. George Newman
President
Broadmoor International, Inc.
120 S. Pikes Peak Avenue
Colorado Springs, CO 80902

Dear Mr. Newman:

In an ever changing market place, creative and aggressive marketing and sales ideas bring profitable growth. For over 20 years my sales marketing skills have helped organize strategies, educate and train personnel, and market products through all steps of the distribution chain. Handling various classifications of retailers, I have first-hand knowledge in developing and implementing innovative approaches to reaching the customer.

A few examples of past achievements:

- Developed and initiated competitive changes in marketing strategies resulting in the launch of 17 new products in 3 months (normal lead time 2 years).

- Directed customers in market analysis, strategy development, establishing sales growth beyond forecasts and expanding the marketplace for the products.

- Increased sales volume 32% in a single year, with consistent quota performance and increased territory growth.

- Introduction of market tests that lead to a new company division and national marketing programs.

- Recovered $750,000 in bad debt while maintaining $3 million business with major dealer.

A copy of my resume is enclosed. My current salary is $45,000 plus bonus. I would be pleased to discuss how my background could be of potential value to your clients. Thank you for your consideration. I look forward to hearing from a member of your staff.

Sincerely,

Nicholas P. Rossini

Enclosure

MARCIANNE R. JONES
12 Scott Street
Wichita, KS 67221
(316) 555-7537 Home
(316) 555-8000 Office

Date

Mr. Vince Olivetti
President
Olivetti & Associates
Two North Hamdon Plaza
Wichita, KS 67202

Dear Mr. Olivetti:

As a Vice President of Human Resources and Assistant Corporate Secretary, I have fifteen years experience working for a Fortune 100 technical manufacturing company. I had "hands-on" experience in administration of benefits, group health, payroll administration, taxes, safety and personnel policies.

You or your clients may be interested in some of my past experience, knowledge and accomplishments.

- Saved over $750,000 in 1991 by developing an "early return to work" program, establishing an ergonomic task force and safety committee.

- Generated $7,000,000 in cash by assisting the cancellation of over funded pension plan, implementing mirror image plan, negotiating annuity contract.

- Implemented program for drug testing, purchased equipment and introduced program to test all new hires and current employees for Carpal Tunnel Syndrome. Saved company about $500,000. Installed HRIS personnel recordkeeping system. Result: $45,000 savings.

- Managed corporate office and moved office twice in last four years. Stayed within budget.

I have a BA degree from Denison University. My resume is enclosed for your review. My current salary is $97,000.

If you have an interest in my background, I would be pleased to meet with you or your client.

Sincerely,

Marcianne R. Jones

Enclosure

Inquiry

ALLEN PAUL MARSDEN
243 Lucerne Drive
Los Angeles, CA 90021
(213) 555-8882

Date

Ms. Rebecca Harper
Director, Information Services
Capital Trust Corporation
1800 W. Chaney Boulevard
Los Angeles, CA 90027

Dear Ms. Harper:

You may be interested in a programmer/analyst with seven years experience. I have had broad exposure to computer languages, hardware, and software.

Some of my past accomplishments include:

- Converted over 100 programs from HP3000 Series 70 MPE/V to Series 960 System MPE/XL.

- Converted data for customer base of 39,000 customers, accounts receivable and order history for two years of data.

- Performed analysis, coding, debugging, testing implementation of over 35 programs for all phases of new order entry system using COBOL for entry screens and COGNOS for reports.

- Streamlined picklist process to run 50% faster which made computer more efficient.

- Acted as user interface for problem solving.

I have an Associate of Applied Science in Data Processing, from Los Angeles City College. Should you have an interest in my background, I would be pleased to meet with you.

Sincerely,

Allen Paul Marsden

Enclosure

ELYSE P. BOUVIER
Six Kelley Court
Gladwyne, PA 19035
(215) 555-8762

Date

Mr. Isaac Wallins
Vice President
Bell & Crown Corporation
777 N. Liberty Place
Philadelphia, PA 19107

Dear Mr. Wallins:

If you are thinking of getting into the world of scanning, I believe I can help you.

My background of over 15 years in the market research area has given me exposure to all aspects of scanning. My most recent project was to review, select and purchase equipment and software to support a retail scanning system. I personally directed the collection and processing of retail consumer data.

My other major accomplishments are in the areas of:

- Negotiations with major retail companies which netted my employer savings between 15 and 22%.

- Management of technical and non-technical personnel with staffs of 10-60 people.

- Developed procedures and programs to review scanning data quality.

- Systems Analysis and programming.

As you can tell, my professional career at the Global Research Company is diversified. My budget responsibilities ranged from $500,000 to $3.5 million with revenue of over $20 million.

I believe my services could be useful to you and I would enjoy meeting with you to discuss possible opportunities. Thank you for your time and consideration.

Sincerely yours,

Elyse P. Bouvier

Enclosure

Specific Openings

WHITNEY MARRS   426 Larsen Court, #2D
                                                 San Francisco, CA 94124

Date

P.O. Box H024
Department 152
San Francisco, CA 94127

Dear Sir or Madam:

In response to your advertisement for an entry-level Accountant in The San Francisco Examiner of January 12, I have enclosed my resume for your review.

I am a recent graduate of Stanford University with a Bachelor of Science in Accounting. My training has not only given me a thorough knowledge of business and accounting practices, but has also taught me the importance of discipline, enthusiasm and old-fashioned hard work in attaining my goals. Throughout my senior year I have been an intern with Slade Jones and Carson, a private accounting firm, where I have been able to apply my learning in a "real world" setting. Besides gaining a broad range of experience in the areas of Accounts Payable, Accounts Receivable, Tax Accounting and Capital Planning, I developed a Lotus spreadsheet to analyze the profitability of the firm's existing accounts.

I believe that I can make an immediate positive contribution to your company. I would enjoy meeting with you to discuss my qualifications in more detail. I look forward to hearing from you shortly.

Sincerely,

Whitney Marrs

Enclosure

JULIA ROJAS

6 Drexel Street
River Forest, IL 60305

Home: (708) 555-9123
Business: (312) 555-8200

Date

Mr. Craig Wynstra
Manager
Spellman Industries, Inc.
One Spellman Parkway
Oak Brook Terrace, IL 60521

Dear Mr. Wynstra:

I am pleased to hear that you are still searching for a consultant to join your team. I have enclosed a copy of my resume for your review.

For the last seven years, I have managed Library and Information Services for the American Dental Association. I have also privately consulted to Dentistry Publishers. In these roles I have developed strong planning and analytical skills as well as sharp management instincts. Last year, I completed my MBA at the Northwestern University Kellogg School of Management. My goal is to move from the not-for-profit sector into the for-profit sector.

I would like to meet with you to discuss my interests and your needs. I look forward to speaking with you further.

Sincerely,

Julia Rojas

Enclosure

W. DANIEL BROPHY
612 Sunset Trail
Ridgewood, New Jersey 07451
(201) 555-4343

Date

Exec-U-Net
21 November Trail
Weston, CT 06883-1505

RE: Exec-U-Net Position Listing G240756

Dear Sir or Madam:

I read your ad for Chief Operating Officer of the "Structural Adhesives Company" outlined in the posting number noted above with great interest. I believe my qualifications would make an outstanding match with the needs and challenges you described.

Throughout my career I have developed high performance organizations in a number of very different settings by building the operations from a solid technical base and leveraging that position for growth. Furthermore, my broad manufacturing background should allow me to learn the adhesives industry quickly.

I would be pleased to meet with you to discuss the position and my qualifications in more detail.

Sincerely yours,

W. Daniel Brophy

Enclosure

Follow-Up

WAYNE BURDICK

3532 W. Champagne Drive
Manchester, New Hampshire 03101

Home: (603) 555-8123
Office: (603) 555-2300

Date

Ms. Shell Whitney
Director of Marketing
Hammel Technology, Inc.
222 East Crown Place
Boston, MA 02186

Dear Ms. Whitney:

Thank you for the brief discussion by phone today and the opportunity to discuss my background and how it might fit with Hammel Technology's needs.

You will see from the enclosed resume that I have a record of achievement in business analysis, marketing and sales within the chemical industry. As Marketing Manager, I had profit responsibility for approximately $50 million worth of business. As Product Marketing Analyst, I was part of the management team developing and implementing marketing and business plans. In addition, I called directly on national and key accounts in the Northeast, increasing sales by $1.1 million in fifteen months. My educational background includes degrees in Chemical Technology and Business Administration.

Should you be interested in an individual with my credentials, experience and proven track record, I would be pleased to meet with you.

Sincerely,

Wayne Burdick

Enclosure

DANIELLE BARNES-DAVISON
102 Elder Brook Terrace
Omaha, NE 68105
(402) 555-3133

Date

Mr. Raymond Grimshaw
National Sales Manager
Harlow Manufacturing Co.
1331 S. Bullock Street
Omaha, NE 68102

Dear Mr. Grimshaw:

I appreciate your willingness to talk with me today over the telephone about the potential administrative assistant opening at your regional sales office. As I mentioned, Marie Quinn suggested that I get in touch with you when she learned that you were thinking about opening this new office. As you requested, enclosed is my resume outlining my experience and qualifications as an administrative assistant.

During my five year tenure at Lutz Industries, I worked as the sole administrative support for a sales staff of four. As the "logistics" member of their sales team, I effectively handled all of the administrative details to allow them to do their thing—make the sale. Some of the many hats that I wore included scheduler, receptionist, word processor and "computer expert," sales assistant . . . and jack-of-all-trades.

Although I realize that you have not yet finalized the details of this position, I would be pleased to meet with you to discuss how my organizational, interpersonal and problem solving skills might benefit your sales organization. I look forward to hearing from you.

Sincerely yours,

Danielle Barnes-Davison

Enclosure

FREDERICK T. COOK
26 Randall Place
Tucson, AZ 85702
(602) 555-9225

Date

Mr. Oliver Chapman
Human Resource Manager
Mitchell International
80 East Kimball Street
Tucson, AZ 85702

Dear Mr. Chapman:

Thank you for discussing the Customer Service Supervisor position with me yesterday. As you requested, I have enclosed my resume outlining my qualifications and experience in Customer Service.

You indicated during our telephone conversation that you are looking for someone with experience managing change and improving corporate quality standards. While at Quick Express, I coordinated the Tucson implementation of the new Fast Mail program, which entailed major reorganization. Subsequently, at ABC Cellular, Inc., I was responsible for initiating and training 16 employees in a quality excellence program. Directing these quality improvement programs has given me invaluable experience, which I would bring to Mitchell.

Again, it was a pleasure to talk with you. Please accept this letter as an indication of my interest in Mitchell International and the position of Customer Service Supervisor. I look forward to hearing from you.

Sincerely,

Frederick T. Cook

Enclosure

Networking

DIANA M. KELPNER
16 Birchwood Lane
Arlington, Virginia 22210
(703) 555-3015

Date

Ms. Rita H. Peacock
Acting Director
Jacobs Foundation for the Arts
229 South Xavier Road
Silver Spring, MD 20907

Dear Rita:

<u>Bravo for Kids: Arts and Education in the Age of Media</u>, my second book for Cromwell Press, is on the press this week and I expect to receive my first copy shortly. Needless to say it is an exciting time for me. With the book finished, it seems appropriate to explore new career opportunities. The last ten and a half years at the National Arts Foundation have been rewarding, so leaving will not be easy. Yet I am ready for new challenges and opportunities.

I have enclosed a copy of my resume. Would you take a look at it to see if you have any suggestions for how to advance my job search? I am particularly interested in any contacts who might put me in touch with other opportunities in the Washington D.C. area.

I enjoyed working with you at the NAF and hope to have the chance to work with you again in another capacity. I will give you a call after the first of the year to see if you have any thoughts or suggesions.

Sincerely,

Diana M. Kelpner

Enclosure

ERNEST C. COHEN
1721 East Hill Street
Minneapolis, MN 55440
(612) 555-6089 Residence
(612) 555-2132 Business

Date

Mr. Hal Swift
Vice President Administration
Mercy Hospital
2251 Jefferson Park Avenue
St. Paul, MN 55104

Dear Hal:

After over 20 years of diversified experience in senior level hospital administration and finance, I am currently investigating alternative career opportunities.

In this regard, I am contacting a select group of friends, acquaintances and business associates to solicit their thoughts regarding my career search. I am receptive to investigating opportunities that might involve relocation, but would have a preference for remaining in the Twin Cities area.

A copy of my resume is enclosed for your review. Should you have any ideas or suggestions, I would be pleased to hear from you.

Best regards,

Ernest C. Cohen

Enclosure

Thank You

Five Kent Way
Brookside Estates, OH 43235
(614) 555-0765

Date

Mr. Terrence Evans
Research and Development Director
Perfect Pet, Inc.
983 S.W. 45th Street
Columbus, OH 43205

Dear Mr. Evans:

Thank you for the opportunity to visit with your team on Wednesday.

The challenge I learned of in the context of Perfect Pet's strategies would appear to be in line with the strengths and skills I have applied in my career up to now. Therefore, I believe I could help accomplish goals necessary in this package development position for:

- cost effective and manufacturable packaging

- environmentally acceptable packaging

- viable packaging for consumer needs

Perfect Pet's focus on prompt action based upon sound technological understanding, development and advancement represents an atmosphere in which I can thrive.

Again Mr. Evans, it was a pleasure to talk with you. Please accept this letter as an indication of my interest in Perfect Pet and the package development position. I will be in contact with Mr. Tzon shortly regarding the next step.

Sincerely,

Thomas C. Esteban

AMANDA G. LLOYD

1124 Dover Cliff Road   Home: (617) 555-2402
Boston, MA 02181   Office: (617) 555-4333

Date

Mr. Marc Kline
Executive Vice President
Chadwick Academy
330 W. Massachusetts Avenue
Boston, MA 02115

Dear Mr. Kline:

Thank you for your consideration for the position of Vice President of Development.

I would also like to express my appreciation for your recent letter informing me of the appointment of Alfred Engel to this position and detailing his extraordinary qualifications. Congratulations on this excellent appointment. I am certain that Mr. Engel will serve you very well in leading the way to financial security.

I am pleased that you are retaining my resume for future reference. Be assured that I would consider it an honor to serve such a venerable institution in an appropriate capacity.

Sincerely,

Amanda G. Lloyd

Broadcast

EDWARD D. O'CONNOR
935 Meridian Street
Hammond, IN 46325
(219) 555-3692

Date

Mr. Steven Carlson
Director, Operations
Wayland Industries, Inc.
229 W. Broadway
Chicago, IL 60612

Dear Mr. Carlson:

In today's economy effective management of warehoused inventory is more important than ever for companies to remain competitive. As a thirteen-year veteran of warehouse management, I have consistently demonstrated the ability to develop and run lean, highly efficient warehouse operations. Some of my accomplishments include:

- Revised warehouse stock location system for $200M inventory that reduced operator cost by $525,000 annually.

- Restructured personnel responsibilities, eliminating 6,000 manpower hours annually while maintaining the highest overall efficiency of all company warehouses.

- Directed warehouse safety program that reduced operation problems by 25%. Used as model for company-wide safety training effort.

My experience encompasses all facets of warehouse operations, including safety management, policy administration, security procedures, personnel development, planning, scheduling and manufacturing. I am a highly motivated, profit-oriented leader with proven communication and problem solving skills.

I would be pleased to spend some time with you to discuss how my background and talents can enhance your company's success.

Sincerely,

Edward D. O'Connor

223 Hollyhock Lane
Providence, RI 02909
(401) 555-9023

May 2, 1992

Mr. James Kilby
President
Charter International, Inc.
One Liberty Plaza
New York, NY 10006

Dear Mr. Kilby:

As a Division General Manager of a large globally-based manufacturing and service business in a $3 billion corporation, I have had the opportunity to restructure, reorganize and reorient businesses towards growth. I have continually risen to the challenge and am proud of the high performance organizations I have developed. Some of my past accomplishments include:

- Restructured two manufacturing businesses in France and England with over $40 million in sales and returned both to profitability in one year.

- Developed six new products and introduced prototypes in one year where historical average had been five.

- Opened new markets in Eastern Europe worth over $300 million and captured nearly $20 million in orders in 1991 and received payment.

- Negotiated and organized numerous international projects worth over $1 billion and delivered significant cash and profits.

In the last twenty years I have proven my abilities as an innovative and progressive leader of businesses in a number of industries and international settings. I would welcome the opportunity to meet you to discuss how I can add value to your organization.

Sincerely yours,

Gerald B. Chatham

Suggested Readings

JOB SEARCH STRATEGIES

Beatty, Richard H. *The New Complete Job Search*. New York: John Wiley & Sons, 1992.

Donaldson, Robert M. *Managing Your Career: How to Choose or Change Your Job*. Salt Lake City, UT: Deseret Book Co., 1985.

STRATEGIES—EXECUTIVES

Foxman, Loretta D. *The Executive Resume Book*. New York: John Wiley & Sons, 1989.

Lucht, John, *Rites of Passage at $100,000+*. New York: The Viceroy Press, 1988.

Swain, Madeleine and Robert Swain. *Out the Organization*. New York: MasterMedia, 1988.

STRATEGIES—RECENT GRADS

Fein, Richard. *Launching Your Business Career*. New York, John Wiley & Sons, 1992.

Lussier, Donald E. *How to Get the "L" Out of Learning*. Orion, MI: Premium Press, 1991.

SELF-ASSESSMENT/CAREER PLANNING

Bolles, Richard Nelson. *What Color Is Your Parachute?* Berkeley, CA: Ten-Speed Press, revised annually.

Burton, Wedemeyer. *In Transition*. New York: Harper Business Press, 1991.

Gale, Barry and Linda Gale. *Discover What You Are Best At: The National Career Aptitude System and Career Directory*. New York: Simon & Schuster, 1982.

Lloyd, Joan. *The Career Decisions Planner*. New York: John Wiley & Sons, 1992.

Sinetar, Marsha. *Do What You Love, The Money Will Follow*. Mahway, NJ: Paulist Press, 1987.

COVER LETTERS

Beatty, Richard H. *The Perfect Cover Letter*. New York: John Wiley & Sons, 1989.

Beatty, Richard H. *175 High-Impact Cover Letters*. New York: John Wiley & Sons, 1992.

INTERVIEWING

Beatty, Richard H. *The Five-Minute Interview*. New York: John Wiley & Sons, 1986.

Fisher, Robert and William Ury. *Getting to Yes*. Boston: Houghton Mifflin, 1981.

Yate, Martin John. *Knock 'Em Dead with Great Answers to Tough Interview Questions*. Holbrook, MA: Bob Adams, Inc., 1988.

Yeager, Neil and Lee Hough. *Power Interviews: Job Winning Tactics from Fortune 500 Recruiters*. John Wiley and Sons, 1990.

UNDERSTANDING THE JOB MARKET

Boyette, Joseph H. and Conn, Henry P. *Workplace 2000: The Revolution Reshaping American Business*. New York: Plume, 1992.

Kleiman, Carol. *The 100 Best Jobs for the 1990's and Beyond*. Chicago: Dearborn Press, 1992.

Wright, John W. *The American Almanac of Jobs and Salaries*. New York: Avon Books, revised annually.

About the Authors

Loretta D. Foxman is President of OI/Cambridge Human Resource Group, a Chicago-based organization consulting firm, and founder of Outplacement International, Inc., the third largest outplacement organization worldwide with over eighty offices in the United States, Canada, and the United Kingdom. She has written and published numerous articles for professional newsletters and magazines in addition to two leading job search books. Her most recent book is *The Executive Resume Book*, John Wiley & Sons, Inc., 1989. A Women of Achievement awardee, Ms. Foxman is a founding director of The International Center for Spouse Relocation Assistance and has served on the board of The United Way of Glencoe and in several committee positions for numerous HR, professional, and civic organizations. Currently she is President of Society of Human Resource Professionals (SHRP), the Chicago chapter of Society for Human Resource Management (SHRM), the largest international human resource management association. Ms. Foxman holds a Masters degree from Columbia University.

Walter L. Polsky is Chairman of Outplacement International, Inc., and CEO of Cambridge Human Resource Group. Prior to founding Cambridge in 1981, Polsky was President of the retainer search firm bearing his name. He has also been involved in human resource management with Continental Grain Company and Bell Laboratories. Polsky and Foxman have cowritten the longest running column on career management and strategic human resource management for *Personnel Journal*, the premier journal in the human resource field. Polsky has a Bachelors degree in general psychology and a Masters degree in counseling.